International Nationalism

First published in 1967, *International Nationalism* discusses the Southern Rhodesian Nationalist Movement and explores how nationalists tried to combine internal with international pressure for self-government. The author provides a well-researched and concise history of various aspects of the Movement—relations with the British government; persuading international institutions; links in Central Africa; headquarters abroad; and the activities of Nkomo—among others. He further explores the relative importance of internal and international activity. A fascinating and scholarly work, this book is a must read for students and researchers of African studies and politics.

I0105105

International Nationalism

The Extra-territorial Relations of Southern Rhodesian African Nationalists

John Day

Routledge
Taylor & Francis Group

First published in 1967
by Routledge & Kegan Paul Ltd

This edition first published in 2024 by Routledge
4 Park Square, Milton Park, Abingdon, Oxon, OX14 4RN

and by Routledge
605 Third Avenue, New York, NY 10017

Routledge is an imprint of the Taylor & Francis Group, an informa business

© John Day 1967

Publisher's Note
The publisher has gone to great lengths to ensure the quality of this reprint but points out that some imperfections in the original copies may be apparent.

Disclaimer
The publisher has made every effort to trace copyright holders and welcomes correspondence from those they have been unable to contact.

A Library of Congress record exists under LCCN: 78362486

ISBN: 978-1-032-89810-0 (hbk)
ISBN: 978-1-003-54469-2 (ebk)
ISBN: 978-1-032-89811-7 (pbk)

Book DOI 10.4324/9781003544692

International Nationalism

The extra-territorial relations of
Southern Rhodesian African nationalists

By John Day
Lecturer in Politics in the
University of Leicester

LONDON
ROUTLEDGE & KEGAN PAUL
NEW YORK: HUMANITIES PRESS

First published 1967
by Routledge & Kegan Paul Ltd
Broadway House, 68–74 Carter Lane
London E.C.4

Printed in Great Britain
by Willmer Brothers Limited

© *John Day 1967*

SBN 7100 5129 8 C
SBN 7100 5118 2 P

General editor's introduction

This series of paper-back monographs is designed primarily to meet the needs of students of government, politics, or political science in Universities and other institutions providing courses leading to degrees. Each volume aims to provide a brief general introduction indicating the significance of its topic, e.g. executives, parties, pressure groups, etc., and then a longer 'case study' relevant to the general topic. First year students will thus be introduced to the kind of detailed work on which all generalizations must be based, while more mature students will have an opportunity to become acquainted with recent original research in a variety of fields. This series will eventually provide a comprehensive coverage of most aspects of political science in a more interesting and fundamental manner than in the large volume which often fails to compensate by breadth what it inevitably lacks in depth.

In recent years political scientists have shown an increasing interest in the developing countries in general and in Africa in particular. The problem of (Southern) Rhodesia is one of the most distinctive, complicated and publicized of all those to have come out of Africa. As in other parts, however the (Southern) Rhodesian Nationalist Movement has tried to combine internal with international pressure for self-government. Mr Day, who has been some time in Salisbury, and has done considerable research into the Nationalist Movement, provides here a concise history of many of the aspects of the Movement and has attempted to estimate the relative importance of internal and international activity. The volume is both fascinating and scholarly and will undoubtedly take its place by the side of the many books already written and yet to be written on this difficult problem.

H.V.W.

Contents

CONTENTS

Acknowledgments

I wish to thank all those who have helped me with the research for this book, in particular, Dr Ahrn Palley and Dr Claire Palley, and those who granted me interviews, Mr Humphry Berkeley, Mr Robert Mugabe, Mr David Mutasa, Mr George Nyandoro, Mr Nelson Samkange, Mr Nathan Shamuyarira, Miss Jane Symonds, and Mr Dick Taverne. The Research Board of the University of Leicester helped to finance the research. Mrs Maureen Thompson typed the manuscript. My wife helped much by checking the manuscript and by offering criticism and encouragement.

Leicester, March 1967   JOHN DAY

9

To My Parents

1

International activities
in the history of nationalism

On 24 October 1964, when Northern Rhodesia became
independent as Zambia, Southern Rhodesia changed
its name to Rhodesia. In this book the country
will be referred to as Southern Rhodesia unless the
reference is to the country exclusively in the
period from 24 October 1964. A similar convention
will be adopted in referring to Northern Rhodesia/
Zambia, Nyasaland/Malawi, and Tanganyika/Tanzania.
Nyasaland was officially Malawi from 6 July 1964.
Nyerere announced that the United Republic of
Tanganyika and Zanzibar had been renamed Tanzania
on 30 October 1964.

In May 1964 Rev. Ndabaningi Sithole, President of ZANU,
one of Southern Rhodesia's two African nationalist parties,
told the party Congress at Gwelo that the African people
would achieve self-government by their own dynamic
action, not, as they had been taught in the past, by the
efforts on their behalf of the United Nations, the United
Kingdom, the Commonwealth, independent African states
or the Afro-Asian bloc. Of course, no one in the nationalist
movement had pretended, as Sithole was rhetorically alleging in order to make a party point, that Southern Rhodesian Africans could or should rely on outside forces to
the exclusion of their own efforts. However, Sithole's asser-

tion suggests the degree to which the hopes of Southern Rhodesian nationalists for political advancement had been geared to expectations of pressure from abroad on the Southern Rhodesian Government. Certainly they have spent much time, energy and money in persuading governments and other institutions outside the country to support their cause. The developing pattern of the nationalists' 'foreign policy' is best understood initially in the context of the general history of the nationalist movement in Southern Rhodesia, because the principal strategies of these extra-territorial relations were adopted in response to challenges made by events and the nationalists' adversaries.

How and why nationalism started in Southern Rhodesia

African nationalism became a significant force in Southern Rhodesia later than in most parts of Africa. In September 1957 a new African National Congress (ANC) was formed by the amalgamation of the new, militant Youth League, drawing its strength initially from the Salisbury townships and dynamically led by George Nyandoro and James Chikerema, with the old, moribund African National Congress, surviving only in Bulawayo, whose chairman was the experienced Joshua Nkomo. In the history of African political organizations in Southern Rhodesia the revitalized ANC was unique, for it succeeded, as no other had done, in creating by vigorous proselytizing a country-wide, mass movement with perpetual momentum. It united the new proletariat of the African townships with the traditional peasantry of the African Reserves in radical protest at the political, economic and social discrimination practised by the European minority against the Africans.

The Europeans have built for themselves a prosperous and advanced society from which they endeavour to

14

exclude Africans except as cheap labour. The Government spends ten times as much on the education of each European child as on the education of each African child. Although Africans outnumber Europeans by eighteen to one, the Land Apportionment Act reserves as much land to the Europeans as to the Africans. The European part contains the main towns and lines of communication, as well as the bulk of the land that is suitable for intensive cultivation. The rapidly expanding African population is short of land while the Europeans leave unused much of the land allocated to them. The average income of a European is ten times the average income of an African in the money economy. Africans often cannot obtain better paid jobs even if they have managed to acquire the necessary skills and when they are allowed to do the same work as Europeans they are frequently paid much less. The colour bar sometimes backed by laws keeps the inhabitants of Southern Rhodesia in two nations. Europeans commonly treat Africans as inferior beings. In 1957 when ANC started the Africans had almost no part in the political system of the territory. A negligible number of Africans qualified on educational and financial grounds for votes and no Africans held seats in the Legislative Assembly.

ANC attacked on a wide front. It had particular success in mobilizing discontent against the Native Land Husbandry Act which the Government was trying to implement at this time. The aim of this Act was to improve African farming practices, but it was carried out without taking account of African resentment at two of its principal parts, the destocking of cattle and the transference of communally held land into farms for individuals. Africans often regarded these measures as fundamental attacks on their livelihood and traditional ways of life.

During its whole existence ANC made its onslaughts

directly on the laws, policy and administration of the Southern Rhodesian Government. It did not try, like its successors, to apply indirect pressure by enlisting the assistance of foreign governments and international institutions.

In February 1959 Sir Edgar Whitehead's Government banned ANC, accusing it of subversion, and detained three hundred and seven of its members. Later it passed a series of laws which strictly controlled political activity. For nearly a year no nationalist organization existed in Southern Rhodesia, but Nkomo, President of the outlawed ANC, who was safely out of the country when the Government swooped, was active abroad in winning international recognition of African grievances in his country. When a new nationalist party, the National Democratic Party (NDP), was formed in January 1960, Nkomo remained out of the country and continued to work overseas from his base in London. He represented NDP abroad until its first annual Congress in October 1960 called him home to become President of the party. Nkomo's international activities during his exile permanently influenced the strategic thinking of the Southern Rhodesian nationalist movement, which henceforth accompanied its domestic politics with efforts abroad.

Nationalist pressure on Britain

NDP adopted the policy, untried by ANC, of pressing the British Government to intervene in Southern Rhodesian politics. The basic cause of this important innovation was the worsening relations of the Southern Rhodesian Government and the nationalists. Some mildly liberal legislation passed by Whitehead's Government after it had destroyed ANC and armed itself with a battery of repressive laws did nothing to assuage the bitter fury of the nationalists. Such measures as permitting hotels to have multi-racial bars did not pacify the nationalists, although politically conscious Africans would have been well pleased with these concessions a few years earlier. Whereas ANC distributed its energies in demanding a wide range of reforms, NDP concentrated its efforts on obtaining soon the single, crucial end of universal franchise. A Government which had declared and demonstrated its hostility to African nationalism faced a new nationalist party aiming to refashion completely and immediately the political system and hence the whole society. During 1960, the first year of NDP's existence, the political temperature rose in Southern Rhodesia. In July and October serious riots by Africans were suppressed by vigorous police action in which eighteen Africans were killed. The chances of constructive discussion between the Government and the nationalists, which looked slim in the days of ANC, seemed negligible in the era of NDP. In this situation and with the example of Nkomo's international deeds in mind NDP worked hard to persuade the British Government to act on its behalf against the Southern Rhodesian Government.

The 1923 Constitution gave Southern Rhodesia a very large measure of self-government in internal affairs, but the British Government had the right, never in fact exercised, to veto legislation which discriminated against the Africans. As Southern Rhodesia remained legally a colony over which the British Government theoretically preserved some control, NDP hoped that they could obtain through the British Government what they could not secure from direct confrontation of the Southern Rhodesian Government. Whitehead, on the other hand, hoped he could persuade the British Government to give up its reserved powers. In fact Whitehead's request for this modification to the Constitution was the immediate cause of NDP's sending a delegation

17

B

to London in April 1960. It urged the nationalist case, opposed Whitehead's proposal, and demanded a constitutional conference. The British Government listened to both sides and did nothing. At first it refused to call a constitutional conference, but by the end of the year changed its mind. Animosity between Whitehead and Nkomo threatened to prevent any formal discussions, but a conference was eventually held early in 1961 in Salisbury under the chairmanship of the Secretary of State for Commonwealth Relations, Duncan Sandys. Whitehead's original request that the British Government's reserved powers should be removed was substantially accepted by the Conference, although other constitutional safeguards for the Africans were provided. The greatest contention was over representation and franchise, in which the nationalists demanded sweeping changes. Eventually all parties, except the right wing Dominion Party, agreed to work a compromise constitution, although 'maintaining their respective positions' (H.M.S.O., Cmnd. 1291, 1961, 6). Under the proposals the Africans could expect to win fifteen seats in a legislative assembly of sixty-five. This fell far short of one man, one vote, which NDP demanded, but was a distinct advance from the existing political system in which very few Africans voted and none sat in the Assembly. However, as soon as the Conference Report appeared, the NDP delegation started to prevaricate and under pressure of severe criticism from within the party began to repudiate the agreement. A special conference of NDP in March 1961 decided to accept the constitutional proposals only under certain conditions which Whitehead's Government would almost certainly not meet. During the next few months NDP leaders fiercely denounced the agreement. In July NDP boycotted the Government referendum on the constitutional proposals and organized its own referendum among Africans, which

18

rejected the proposals. Once the new Constitution was introduced, NDP and its successor ZAPU did all they could to discourage Africans from registering as voters or taking part in elections. Once they decided to go back on their agreement to the constitutional proposals, NDP sent ambassadors to argue with the British Government, which gave them no satisfaction.

Although NDP had not handled the 1961 Conference very skilfully, the nationalists have made it a major point of their policy since 1961 to insist that the British Government should suspend the Constitution and call another constitutional conference. The British Government's policy at first was to insist that the new Constitution should be the basis of political development, in spite of the nationalists' constant pressure to scrap it and their persistent refusal to work under its aegis. Only under pressure of demands for independence by the Rhodesian Front Government, which has been in power since December 1962, did the British Government consider any alterations in the 1961 Constitution. The British Government was prepared to grant independence under certain conditions, which would have entailed amending the 1961 Constitution. This proposal by the British Government came not as a result of the nationalists' pressure, but through the British Government's attempts to bargain with the Southern Rhodesian Government.

Difficulties at home and strategies abroad

Besides direct application to the British Government, the nationalists have tried to recruit allies who might push the British and Southern Rhodesian Governments towards the nationalists' goal. Much of their variegated international activity has been employed in encouraging foreign parties, foreign governments and international institutions to protest against the policies of the British and Southern Rhodesian Governments.

Nkomo set the example in his exile from 1958 to 1960 of seeking the support of those who opposed imperialism around the world. He and other Southern Rhodesian nationalists have especially cultivated friendly relations with independent African states. In several foreign capitals the nationalists have posted permanent representatives. Complementary to this policy has been assiduous attendance by the nationalists at Pan-African and Afro-Asian conferences. Their lobbyists have worked hard, too, at the conferences of Commonwealth Prime Ministers in London. These efforts to win sympathetic friends were usually successful, although neither the British nor the Southern Rhodesian Government significantly changed its position because of its global unpopularity.

The greatest of the nationalists' empty victories was to enlist the United Nations among its supporters. The campaign in New York started seriously in February 1962 and showed distinct results by the end of the year. The submission by the nationalists of their case to the United Nations began when it had become quite clear that the British Government would not merely, because of the nationalists' demands, call another constitutional conference and scrap the 1961 Constitution. Concentration of the nationalists' efforts on the United Nations coincided with the appearance of a new party, the Zimbabwe African People's Union (ZAPU). (Zimbabwe is the nationalists' name for Southern Rhodesia.) ZAPU immediately replaced NDP when that organization was banned in December 1961 for alleged violence. Violence by Africans, principally against other Africans, continued after the suppression of NDP, and in September 1962 the Government, blaming ZAPU for this, ended its official life. ZAPU continued

20

underground and overseas, its leaders being particularly active at the United Nations just after the party was banned. Since then the nationalists have at irregular intervals urged the United Nations both formally and informally to help their cause. The United Nations have frequently responded by passing resolutions supporting the nationalists' stand on Southern Rhodesia.

In achieving the nationalists' ultimate aims in Southern Rhodesia their approaches to the United Nations, to the British Government, to Pan-African conferences and to independent African states have been equally ineffective. This failure has not dampened the nationalists' enthusiasm, blunted their persistence, or deterred them from continuing for the most part with the same strategies and tactics. In their dealings with both the British Government and the United Nations they started with concentrated activity, 1960-1 with one, 1962-3 with the other. The failure of these first big efforts to bring striking improvements in the Africans' position in Southern Rhodesia did not lead the nationalists to abandon the basic strategies of appealing to London and New York, although their activities became more sporadic.

When ZAPU was banned in September 1962 Sithole under Nkomo's instruction stayed out of the country to run the party's overseas affairs. From mid-1962, when ZAPU was expecting the Government to strike at it, Nkomo was seriously considering the possibility of transferring most of the leaders to a headquarters out of the country if the party was banned. Seven months after the ban in April 1963 nearly the whole executive of the party suddenly moved from Southern Rhodesia to Dar-es-Salaam. Nkomo seems to have thought that the leaders could plan the future better in exile under a friendly government than under the surveillance at home of a hostile state. Also, in December

21

1962 the first election under the new Constitution had returned the Rhodesian Front to power, and this Government was working to secure independence. The nationalists feared that complete severance from Britain would prevent any improvement in the Africans' already bad conditions. The ZAPU executive's flight to Tanganyika made it possible to form an African government-in-exile if the Southern Rhodesian Government risked a unilateral declaration of independence (UDI).

In July 1963 dissatisfaction with Nkomo's leadership amongst some ZAPU leaders led to a split in the nationalist movement which has remained unhealed. The ZAPU executive returned to Southern Rhodesia and two new parties emerged in August 1963, the Zimbabwe African National Union (ZANU), the dissidents led by Sithole, and the People's Caretaker Council (PCC), the loyalists under Nkomo. Abroad PCC still retained the name ZAPU. Civil war between PCC and ZANU was the outstanding feature of the nationalist movement during the period when the Government tolerated their existence, between August 1963 and August 1964.

The same policies overseas were pursued after the split as before, but each of the two parties duplicated the work of the other. In April 1964 the Government, now led by Ian Smith, restricted Nkomo to the remote area of Gonakudzingwa. Soon a group of four PCC leaders, including Nyandoro and Chikerema, the pioneers of the Youth League and ANC, in detention from 1959 to 1963, formed a permanent headquarters in exile in Lusaka. Thus some of the experienced nationalist leaders remained free to continue the fight abroad as the Government restricted more and more of the leaders in Southern Rhodesia.

Few were free in August 1964 when the Government banned both PCC and ZANU, again for violence, and re-

22

stricted the remaining leaders, thus paralysing nationalist political life in Southern Rhodesia. Since that time the Government has continued its iron grip on the nationalist movement. The most influential leaders have never been released and no new nationalist party has been born. Since the ban on PCC and ZANU no new ideas for political activity abroad have emerged. Yet the extreme difficulties under which nationalism labours in Southern Rhodesia and the impotence of its leaders confined in Government camps have made the international activities of the Lusaka group and other nationalists in exile relatively more important than in the period when some political organization was possible at home.

In November 1965 the Rhodesian Government declared independence unilaterally. The British Government did not recognize this independence and treated the Rhodesian Ministers as rebels. UDI did not mark a watershed for the nationalists at home or abroad. The Government had already snuffed out all expressions of nationalism in Rhodesia except uncoordinated attacks on property. If the nationalists had been able to set up a government-in-exile and had it recognized by many governments, UDI might even have strengthened the nationalists' position. In fact they went on as before. They asked for British military intervention against the illegal regime in Rhodesia and for the creation by Britain of a democratic political system to replace it. But they had since 1960 demanded British intervention, if necessary with force, and the introduction of majority rule. For years the nationalists had predicted an African uprising in Southern Rhodesia, especially if independence was declared unilaterally, but this did not happen at UDI and has not happened since. Sporadic violence has continued and some bands of guerilla fighters have been in action against security forces.

This small scale guerilla warfare has been organized from abroad. Rhodesian nationalists in Zambia have helped to send foreign arms and trained guerillas into Rhodesia. But the planning of violence by foreign based Southern Rhodesian nationalists started long before UDI, in the middle of 1962. For several years some independent African states from the north and some Communist countries have trained Rhodesian Africans in guerilla warfare and provided war materials for their use. The Government used the existence of several hundred Rhodesian nationalists across the border in Zambia to help to justify declarations of emergency in November 1965 and afterwards at three monthly intervals, but neither the threat nor the achievement of these revolutionaries infiltrating into Rhodesia from Zambia has forced the Government to concede anything to the nationalists. Like all the other methods tried by the nationalists at home and abroad the deeds of these foreign trained fighters have not brought the nationalists nearer to political power.

With the broad strategies of the nationalists' international relations placed in the context of the general history of the movement, we shall now examine more closely each field of foreign endeavour.

2

Relations with the British Government

Why the nationalists appealed to the British Government and what they demanded

The relations of the Southern Rhodesian nationalists with the British Government have been significantly different from those of other nationalists with the metropolitan power. Anti-imperialist movements within the British Empire have commonly exerted pressure on the home government in Britain as well as on the government in the colony, but whereas in ordinary Colonial Office colonies, like Northern Rhodesia, the nationalists were dealing with one political system with its headquarters in London and with a local authority in Lusaka, in Southern Rhodesia the nationalists have faced two separate governments with independent powers, either of which might conceivably be persuaded to act in the nationalists' interests without the concurrence of the other.

Since 1923 Southern Rhodesia has enjoyed almost complete internal self-government. Under the 1923 Constitution certain classes of legislation were subject to the discretion of the British Government. It had reserved powers over constitutional amendments and most laws which subjected

Africans to conditions or restrictions not applying to Europeans. Also, the British Government could disallow any law within a year of its receiving the Governor's assent. In practice the British Government did not avail itself of its constitutional rights, although their existence and resulting discussions of proposed legislation between the British and the Southern Rhodesian Governments affected to some extent the laws presented to the Southern Rhodesian legislature. In 1961 the British Government recognized an established convention not to legislate for Southern Rhodesia on any matters within the competence of the Southern Rhodesian legislature, except with its own consent. Yet the British Government retained its formal sovereignty.

The strange relationship of the British Government with the Southern Rhodesian Government largely explains the energy expended by Southern Rhodesian nationalists in trying to move the British Government and also, paradoxically, their difficulties and failures in doing this. Because of the racial policies of Southern Rhodesian Governments the British Government would not relinquish its tenuous sovereignty over the territory, but, having granted responsible government to the white minority, would not intervene to change those racial policies. The refusal of the British Government to give Southern Rhodesia independence until the Africans had a secure place in the political system encouraged the nationalists to appeal to the British Government for help. The unwillingness of the British Government to do anything about Southern Rhodesia to which the Southern Rhodesian Government had not consented doomed the nationalists to endless frustration.

The Africans' demands to the British Government have constantly assumed that Southern Rhodesia is a normal British colony in which Britain has the right and the power to intervene if she chooses. For example, when Whitehead

in March 1959 was introducing into the Southern
Rhodesian Legislative Assembly new laws to control strictly
political activity in the territory, Nkomo called on the
British Government to veto this legislation. He did not
recognize the validity of the convention by which the
British Government denied itself the right, offered by the
1923 Constitution, to intervene in the internal affairs of
Southern Rhodesia. As a consequence of this attitude the
nationalists have often appealed to the British Government
to rescind Southern Rhodesian laws, especially those limit-
ing political activity, to release nationalists detained or restricted by the Southern Rhodesian Government, and to
remove bans on nationalist parties imposed by that Government. The nationalists' spokesmen have directly or indirectly protested to the British Government at each action
of the Southern Rhodesian Government which seriously en-
dangered their position. They objected, for instance, in
1964 to the Rhodesian Government's claiming that it had
adequately consulted African opinion on the proposed independence by holding an *indaba* at Dombashawa of Chiefs
and Headmen.

More far-reaching than such complaints have been the
nationalists' continuous demands that the British Government drastically overhaul the whole Southern Rhodesian
political system. Since the nationalists turned their attention to the British Government their principal demands,
monotonously reiterated, have been for one man, one vote,
and a constitutional conference at which this would be
introduced. When NDP decided that the 1961 constitutional
Conference had from their point of view been a failure
they insisted on a new conference. Frequently linked with
the central demand for universal franchise have been requests that the British Government should suspend the
present constitution and take over in Southern Rhodesia,

27

if necessary with force, until the new constitution bringing majority rule came into effect. Year after year these insistent requests have been accompanied by warnings that failure to do as the nationalists wanted would lead to immediate and catastrophic violence, as the patience of the Africans in Southern Rhodesia has (allegedly) been running out. Recently the nationalists have sometimes claimed that this prophesied violence has erupted.

Meetings with British Ministers

The nationalists have repeated their entreaties over and over again to an almost permanently impervious British Government. They have made many efforts to meet British Ministers to explain their case personally. The first attempts to speak directly to the British Government were made in 1960 by the newly formed NDP. When Harold Macmillan, the British Prime Minister, visited Salisbury in January 1960, the party applied unsuccessfully to see him. Whether NDP saw Lord Home, the Commonwealth Secretary, when he came to Southern Rhodesia in February 1960, is not clear, although it certainly submitted a memorandum to him. This opposed the removal of the British Government's reserved powers which Whitehead was seeking. In April Whitehead's visit to London for further discussions of this question with Home induced NDP to send some of its leaders to argue the party's case. The President, Michael Mawema, headed a delegation which also included Moton Malianga, the Deputy President, and Leopold Takawira, a recruit to NDP from the moderate, inter-racial Capricorn Africa Society. These three from Southern Rhodesia were accompanied by three fellow countrymen living in England, Bernard Chidzero, a political scientist, Enoch Dumbutshena, an ex-schoolmaster studying law, and Paul

Mushonga, who had been arrested as an ANC leader, but released through ill health. Home at first refused to meet the delegation and, after he had relented and listened to it, refused to arrange the constitutional conference they suggested. He did, however, assure the delegation that the British Government would not suddenly abandon its reserved powers. In July 1960 Nkomo, who had lived in London since March 1959, but who had been away in April 1960, tried unsuccessfully to speak to Macmillan and Home about the disturbances going on in Southern Rhodesia. When Duncan Sandys, who succeeded Home at the Commonwealth Relations Office, went to Southern Rhodesia in September 1960, an NDP delegation of Mawema, Malianga, Takawira, Herbert Chitepo, the first African barrister in Southern Rhodesia and an NDP National Councillor, and Enos Nkala, the Deputy National Secretary, had talks with him.

Later in the year NDP was able to win something from the British Government, because 1960 was the year in which the Federation of Rhodesia and Nyasaland, of which Southern Rhodesia was a member, was being reviewed. The British Government arranged for a conference to be held in London in December 1960 to discuss the future of the Federation in the light of the recommendations made by the Monckton Commission, which during 1960 reviewed the state of the Federation. NDP was not particularly interested in the Federal Review Conference, because, like nationalists in Northern Rhodesia and Nyasaland, it wished to end Federation as quickly as possible, not discuss how it could be modified. However, NDP believed that it had a right to be represented in the Southern Rhodesian delegation to the Federal Review Conference and resented its exclusion by Whitehead, who justified his refusal to invite Nkomo (from October, President of NDP) by asserting that he had no qualification. NDP was still hoping that a territorial conference would be held near the time of the Federal Review Conference, particularly as a similar arrangement had been made for Northern Rhodesia. To push the claims of NDP Nkomo, who had been home only a week after his long exile, returned to London at the end of November. If he were not offered a seat at the Federal Review Conference or could not obtain a territorial conference, he would try to embarrass the Southern Rhodesian and British Governments. It seems probable that the British Government feared that the nationalists from the two northern territories would boycott the Federal Review Conference if their allies from the south were refused seats in Whitehead's delegation and if there were no conference on Southern Rhodesia. Soon after Nkomo's return to London at the end of November a conference on Southern Rhodesia was announced and Whitehead offered NDP two seats on his delegation to the Federal Review Conference. Probably Sandys persuaded Whitehead to make these concessions. NDP expressed dissatisfaction with the size of their representation and Nkomo made this an inflammatory issue throughout the Federal Review Conference. His agitation about it culminated in his walking out of the Conference. Whitehead was offended at this and withdrew his consent to the presence of NDP at the territorial Conference. This underlines the slight authority of the British Government over the Southern Rhodesian Government. The territorial Conference started in London without NDP. Nkomo, who had discussed NDP's position with various British Ministers at Chequers, when he was the Prime Minister's guest there, and in two interviews with Sandys, eventually met Whitehead about NDP's complaint. The result was a compromise. Nkomo wrote to Whitehead regretting that his walking out of the Federal Review Conference might be interpreted as a discourtesy to Whitehead.

30

Nkomo also issued a joint statement with Whitehead condemning political violence in Southern Rhodesia (some violence had broken out in Salisbury and the Government blamed NDP supporters for it). Finally, NDP were to be represented at the territorial Conference to be reconvened in Salisbury in the new year.

The very holding of the Conference on Southern Rhodesia was a victory for NDP, who recognized this as their great opportunity for at last making a political advance. At the Conference NDP enjoyed formally equal status with the Southern Rhodesian Government party and the two other European parties. At first deadlock seemed highly probable about the crucial questions of franchise and representation, for the Africans wanted one man, one vote, while the European parties wanted less radical changes from the existing system which gave the Europeans power. To try to overcome the difficulties, Sandys, the chairman of the Conference, saw each of the delegations privately. He saw the NDP delegation four times. It consisted of two members, Nkomo and Sithole, the National Treasurer, with two advisers, George Silundika, the Secretary General, and Chitepo. From these informal meetings and further formal discussions a compromise emerged by which the Africans would for the first time have some seats in the Legislative Assembly, but only enough to make them a weak minority. Sandys asked the NDP delegation specifically to help draft the wording of that part of the Conference Report in which the various parties agreed to give the compromise constitution, not properly satisfactory to any of them, a fair trial. In spite of the NDP delegation's participation in phrasing this part of the Report, the franchise and representation proposals failed to satisfy strong and vocal elements in NDP. The members of the delegation made little attempt, at least in public, to defend the proposals and pretended that they had agreed to less than they had. A statement by Nkomo a day after the Conference Report appeared made Sandys check with NDP that they had not changed their position. He received a placatory assurance from Silundika, but NDP moved steadily towards complete hostility to the new Constitution. This led to attempts by the leaders to re-open discussions with the British Government, which, having secured an agreement at the Conference, would not yield to the nationalists' pressure for revising it. Within a week of the end of the Conference Nkomo flew to London and had three meetings with Sandys, but the British Government remained adamant. In mid-May Sandys returned to Salisbury to work out the details of the new Constitution in another conference. NDP now insisted that the repeal of the Land Apportionment Act should be written into the Constitution, but Sandys refused to do more than elaborate the broad agreement reached at the February Conference. Near the start of the new conference NDP walked out and did not return. Sandys invited the NDP leaders to meet him. Nkomo, Malianga, Sithole, Chitepo and Robert Mugabe, the National Secretary for Information and Publicity, saw Sandys, but deadlock ensued, as he would not call another constitutional conference at which fundamentals could be discussed. In June 1961 NDP sent Malianga to London to present a petition to Macmillan asking for what it called a genuine constitutional conference and denouncing the February Conference as a conspiracy between the British and Southern Rhodesian Governments. Macmillan refused to see Malianga, but suggested that he saw Sandys, which he declined. In August 1961 an NDP delegation of Nkomo, Malianga and Dumbutshena obtained an interview with the Duke of Devonshire, Under-Secretary of State for Commonwealth Relations (Sandys was away), and presented to him the result of the NDP referendum which rejected the con-

32

stitutional proposals. Devonshire replied that the Africans could not be given control in Southern Rhodesia, because the complex industrial organization there must not be placed in inexperienced hands.

After the period of these few months which followed the constitutional Conference of February 1961, the meetings of the nationalists with members of the British Government became sporadic. In December 1961 Nkomo took advantage of being present with Sandys at the Tanganyika independence celebrations to ask the British Minister, without effect, to intervene in Southern Rhodesia to remove the ban recently imposed by the Government on NDP. When Butler, as the Minister responsible for Central African Affairs, visited Southern Rhodesia in May 1962, NDP's successor, ZAPU, refused to see him because he considered the constitution to be a closed issue. When Butler planned to return to Central Africa in January 1963, Nkomo at first stated that he would not see Butler unless the ban on ZAPU, imposed the previous September, was lifted. However, Nkomo was prone to changes of mind and in fact he led a delegation which met Butler. The delegation consisted of: Nkomo, President of ZAPU; Chikerema, Secretary for Public Relations, who had recently been released after four years' captivity for his leadership of ANC; Washington Malianga, brother of Moton, and National Secretary; Mugabe, National Secretary for Information and Publicity; and Takawira, Secretary for Pan-African and External Affairs. Predictably they asked Butler to remove the ban on ZAPU and to call a constitutional conference. Equally predictably Butler told ZAPU that the British Government could not intervene in Southern Rhodesian affairs, and no constitutional conference was called. The ZAPU delegation were reported to have found Butler more amenable than Sandys, but still unforthcoming. Butler asked to see

33

ZAPU again before he left and had them prepare a memorandum on their grievances.

In March 1963 the British Government held talks in London with the Governments of Southern and Northern Rhodesia about future relations between their countries. Nkomo was not invited to these talks, but following his own example of November 1960, preceded the official delegations to London. Butler agreed to see Nkomo before the official conference began. Nkomo, with Chikerema, Dumbutshena and J. M. Chirimbani from the ZAPU London office, made the customary demands and urged British intervention. He also protested against the Preservation of Constitutional Government Bill, being introduced by the new Rhodesian Front Government, which would impose legal restrictions on the operations of the nationalists abroad. In New York a few days later Nkomo said he had given the British Government twenty-four hours to answer his demand for a repeal of the security laws or be responsible for the explosive outcome. Butler ignored this and passed on Nkomo's suggestions to the Southern Rhodesian Government.

In June 1963 Takawira, Secretary for Pan-African and External Affairs, went to London to speak to Butler, as the nationalists were concerned about the talks between the British and Southern Rhodesian Governments on independence, for which the Rhodesian Front was pressing strongly. Takwira, accompanied by Dumbutshena and Noel Mukono, ZAPU's new London representative, saw Butler and afterwards claimed that he had promised that a conference would be held on Southern Rhodesia, to which the nationalists would be invited, after the Victoria Falls Conference, which was to disccuss the dismantling of the Federation. This was officially denied.

After the split in the nationalist movement the anti-Nkomo party, ZANU, sent Mugabe, their Secretary General, to London in September 1963 to speak on their behalf to Butler. In addition to making the standard demands Mugabe expressed the Africans' anger that the British Government was allocating so formidable a part of the Federal armed forces to Southern Rhodesia on the dissolution of Federation at the end of 1963. The British Government remained unmoved.

Early in 1964 Nyandoro, Secretary General of Nkomo's PCC/ZAPU, had a fruitless interview with Richard Hornby, the Under-Secretary of State for Commonwealth Relations. When the Labour Party came into office in October 1964 it gave the Rhodesian Africans no more satisfaction than the Conservative Governments which had ruled during the lifetime of the modern nationalist movement. A ZANU delegation, Simpson Mtambanengwe, Secretary for International Affairs, and Mukono, Deputy National Secretary, travelled to London in December 1964 with one of its principal objectives to see Arthur Bottomley, the new Commonwealth Secretary. The delegation complained that Bottomley refused to see them, although they did speak to Cledwyn Hughes, the Minister of State for Commonwealth Relations. When Bottomley visited Rhodesia in February 1965, seeking to avert a crisis over the Rhodesian Government's demands for independence and its threats of declaring it unilaterally, he spoke to Nkomo who was in restriction, and to five of his lieutenants, but was not permitted to see Sithole who was in prison, although he saw five other ZANU leaders, including Takawira, the Deputy President. The nationalists made the customary protests and demands. Bottomley replied with vague, non-committal statements. In June 1965 Nyandoro, PCC/ZAPU Secretary General, spoke to Bottomley in London and in September 1965 Nelson Samkange, the party's London representative, saw Bottomley again. The British Government continued to preserve the existing situation, conceding neither independence to the Rhodesian Government nor majority rule to the nationalists. The Labour Government was practising the pragmatic conservatism of its Conservative predecessors.

In October 1965 the Prime Minister, Harold Wilson, visited Rhodesia himself in an attempt to prevent a UDI which looked ever more likely. Nkomo and Sithole with their main supporters were brought from restriction to see Wilson in Salisbury. Wilson's main purposes in the interviews he had with the nationalists, three with PCC, three with ZANU, were: to convince them that the British Government would not intervene militarily in Rhodesia to suspend or amend the 1961 Constitution, to impose majority rule, or to deal with a UDI; to inform them that the British Government did not believe that majority rule could come immediately or soon; and to urge them to unite and to work the 1961 Constitution. On this occasion, as during Bottomley's visit, the British Government sought out the nationalists, but this implied no willingness to make concessions to the nationalists, who, restricted and divided, were a weaker force than ever before. Both Sithole and Nkomo had long discussions with Wilson, but his statements and suggestions were completely unacceptable to them. The nationalists repeated their demands, seeking what Wilson was refusing, and the result was the inevitable stalemate. The gap between the British Government and the nationalists was as unbridgeable as that between the British Government and the Rhodesian Government. The difference was that the Rhodesian Government had power.

On 11 November 1965 Rhodesia declared UDI. Before it the British Government had not intervened because of constitutional scruples and political expediency. After UDI only the second motive operated. The British Government continued to ignore the nationalists' demands. In September 1966 Herbert Bowden, the Commonwealth Secretary, while in Salisbury exploring the possibilities of compromise with the rebel regime, was refused permission to see Nkomo and Sithole, but did speak to some members of PCC and ZANU.

Pressure on the British Government by methods other than personal confrontation

The personal pleas of the nationalists to the British Government have been supplemented by many memoranda, letters and telegrams. When the NDP delegation met Home in April 1960, for example, it presented a twelve page memorandum. Rather unusually, Butler, after he had seen the ZAPU delegation in January 1963, solicited from them a document listing their grievances. Between interviews with British Ministers the nationalists have intermittently kept their views before the British Government by post. A few cases will ilustrate this. In 1964 Chikerema and Nyandoro sent telegrams to the Prime Minister, Sir Alec Douglas-Home, from Dar-es-Salaam and Lusaka. They informed him of dangers which allegedly threatened Nkomo's life at the restriction camp in Gonakudzingwa. Later in the year after PCC had been banned, Chikerema wrote a letter to Douglas-Home in which he attacked the Southern Rhodesian Government's intention to consult the Chiefs about independence, called for an end to repressive measures against the nationalists, accused the police of brutality against Africans and made the standard constitutional demands.

An exceptional form of direct pressure on the British Government was the presentation in May 1963 to the British High Commissioner in Salisbury for forwarding to London of a petition opposing independence for Southern

Rhodesia under the 1961 Constitution. This was organized after ZAPU was banned, and during part of the time when signatures were being collected most of the ZAPU executive were out of the country. The organization was the work of Nathan Shamuyarira, a journalist, and Josiah Chinamano, a headmaster, neither of whom had held high office in the nationalist parties (although both were to attain political eminence, after the split, in opposing parties). About two hundred thousand Africans signed the petition, much less than the original goal, but, as the organizers pointed out, more than the number of registered voters.

Although the direct contacts between the British Government and the nationalists have been rather infrequent and irregular, work to exert indirect pressure on the British Government by creating a body of British opinion sympathetic to the nationalists' cause has been sustained more or less continuously since Nkomo came to England in 1959. Spreading their views in England has been particularly important to the nationalists because of the competing versions of Southern Rhodesian affairs which have been circulating. The Southern Rhodesian Government issued its own propaganda through Rhodesia House in London until UDI. Voice and Vision, an advertising agency, was employed by the Federal Government to popularize its policies. European interests in Southern Rhodesia were championed by the Friends of Rhodesia till mid-1965 and by the Anglo-Rhodesian Society since then.

The nationalists have produced several duplicated periodicals from their London offices, which presented slanted news on Southern Rhodesia spiced with impassioned comment. NDP published *Radar* from 1960 to 1961, which was succeeded in 1962 by ZAPU's *Spear* in a similar format, with Nkomo on the cover staring out from a map of Southern Rhodesia. From 1964 to 1965 ZANU produced

Voice of Zimbabwe and PCC/ZAPU competed with *Zimbabwe Review*, which from January 1966 has come out in newspaper format. This periodical propaganda was directed partly at a limited English public and partly at Southern Rhodesian Africans living in Britain. The intention was to inform and inspire these temporary exiles in the hope that they would convert to the nationalist cause those Englishmen they met. The often virulent tone of these periodicals was more calculated to maintain the fervour of the faithful than win the favour of the uncommitted. In addition to periodicals, NDP in London published pamphlets, *The African Case* (on reserved powers) and *Southern Rhodesia: Historical Background to the African Political Struggle*, which both appeared in 1960.

Probably a more effective way of reaching the British public was through the national press. The Southern Rhodesian nationalists fully exploited this medium by making frequent press statements and at crucial times holding press conferences. This has resulted in good coverage by the 'quality' newspapers, which presumably are read by those who make political decisions on Southern Rhodesia. The nationalists also wrote letters to these newspapers. In February 1964 Nyandoro had an article in the *Spectator*. Occasionally the nationalists reached a wider audience by broadcasting. In 1965 and 1966, for instance, several of them appeared on the BBC television programme *Twenty-Four Hours* and Nyandoro spoke on the radio. The nationalists took every opportunity to address meetings of potential sympathizers. Nkomo probably had the biggest audiences in 1959 when he made speeches in the Royal Albert Hall and in Central Hall, London.

Much of the nationalists' activity in London is aimed at those who have access to or can harry Government Ministers. For example, K. I. D. Mutasa, the ZANU representa-

39

tive from 1964 to 1966 saw civil servants at the Commonwealth Relations Office. The more usual form of lobbying has been frequent visits to selected sympathetic M.P.s from both sides of the House, like Dick Taverne in the Labour Party and Humphry Berkeley from the Conservative Party. None of the nationalists addressed the Commonwealth Committee of the Parliamentary Labour Party and on only one occasion did one of them (Nkomo) speak to the parallel Conservative Committee. In March 1963 Nkomo saw Harold Wilson, then Leader of the Opposition, who promised, according to Nkomo, that a Labour Government would introduce a new constitution for Southern Rhodesia.

Various English organizations helped the Southern Rhodesian nationalists in their London political work. Nkomo approached the Africa Bureau, which arranged press conferences for him. The Movement for Colonial Freedom provided ZAPU with a small office in their dingy house near King's Cross Station. Several times they gave the Southern Rhodesian nationalists the opportunity to speak at meetings they organized.

The organization in London

The nationalists in London who were trying by various means to gain British Government assistance were of two types, special visitors from Africa and officials resident in London. The continuity achieved in propaganda and lobbying resulted from the work of the parties' London representatives, who were responsible for producing the periodicals and for maintaining contact with certain journalists and M.P.s.

A formal organization was first set up when Nkomo had been in exile almost a year. In January 1960 he announced the formation of the Southern Rhodesian African Congress

Committee Abroad, which later became the overseas headquarters of NDP and its London office. Nkomo led the organization and was helped by Dumbutshena. During 1960 Nkomo was often abroad on political visits, so that Dumbutshena became the permanent NDP link in London. When Nkomo returned to Southern Rhodesia in November 1960 after NDP had elected him President, Takawira, who had briefly been President of NDP himself, took over in London.

After the constitutional Conference of January to February 1961 Takawira caused a dramatic crisis in the party. With Dumbutshena and Mushonga, who had been in the NDP delegation to Home the previous April, and also worked for the London office, Takawira sent a telegram from London to NDP headquarters in Salisbury and to some local branches in Southern Rhodesia, fiercely denouncing as a betrayal the constitutional proposals to which the delegation led by Nkomo had consented. He described the agreement as 'diabolical and disastrous'. Copies of the explosive telegram Takawira gave to the press, thus ensuring wide publicity for the division in the party. The NDP council suspended Takawira, not for his opinions, which were rapidly becoming those of the party, but for the disloyal way he expressed them. Nkomo returned to London to 'discipline' Takawira, who was, however, pardoned at the party Congress a month later.

He remained in charge in London until early 1962 when he returned to Southern Rhodesia. The London office was then run by Chirimbani, who was not, unlike Nkomo and Takawira, high in the party hierarchy, although he had been head of the NDP office in Tanganyika.

The independence of the London office was again demonstrated in September 1962. Nkomo, in Lusaka when ZAPU was banned, suddenly went to Dar-es-Salaam, al-

41

though some people felt that he was doing the nationalist cause a disservice by not returning to Southern Rhodesia. Chirimbani went out to Dar-es-Salaam to advise Nkomo to return to Southern Rhodesia. To support his case for Nkomo's return home. Chirimbani urged the view on Nkomo that Butler, the British Minister responsible for Central Africa, might not receive Nkomo if he came to London, on the pretext that he had lost the confidence of his supporters. The London representative felt that he was capable of presenting ZAPU's demands to the British Government.

Mukono, who replaced Chirimbani in May 1963, supported the rebels against Nkomo that July, thus repeating the pattern of February 1961 when Takawira had denounced the leader from London. Later ZANU was represented in London by Mtambanengwe, who, like Dumbutshena, was studying law, and who at the time of the revolt was President of the Zimbabwe Students Union in London. The next ZANU representative was Mutasa, who also did his political duties part-time because he too was a student. (He was unable to bring out *Voice of Zimbabwe* in February 1965 because of his examinations.) Since June 1966 Frank Ziyambi has been ZANU's man in London.

PCC/ZAPU seem not to have had a resident official in London for some time after the split. At first it may have been difficult to find a Southern Rhodesian African already living in London who could do the job, because most of them were students, who tended at that time to support Sithole's breakaway. During 1964 PCC/ZAPU did political work in London solely through the visits of executive members from Africa. Nyandoro went to London in April for medical treatment and returned there in July for the Commonwealth Prime Ministers' Conference with Silundika and J. Z. Moyo, colleagues at the headquarters in Lusaka.

Moyo was back in September, and Chikerema, also resident in Lusaka, later in 1964. Not until February 1965 did PCC/ZAPU send a permanent representative, Nelson Samkange, who had recently graduated in Economics from the University College in Salisbury. Unlike Mutasa, his ZANU rival, Samkange worked full-time for his party from the London office. PCC/ZAPU were inevitably handicapped in what they could do in London when they depended on occasional visitors, although they did manage to produce two numbers of *Zimbabwe Review* before Samkange arrived.

Since 1965 PCC/ZAPU and ZANU have both had London offices, each attacking the other while advocating the same policies on Rhodesia. The nationalist organization in England has not changed, but has been duplicated.

3
Persuading international institutions

To supplement their efforts to influence the British Government by direct contact and through British public opinion the Southern Rhodesian nationalists have spent much energy in persuading the United Nations and the Commonwealth to press the United Kingdom on the Southern Rhodesian problem. It was hoped that the British Government would be sensitive to the expressed opinions of these international institutions of which it was a prominent member. When the Commonwealth and the United Nations did act as the nationalists' advocates, however, the British Government was embarrassed but not influenced. Because the organs of the United Nations are in frequent session, whereas representatives of the Commonwealth states meet formally together only once a year at most, the British Government has more often on the Southern Rhodesian question had to defy the United Nations than to manipulate the Commonwealth. But the hostility of a majority of the Commonwealth countries over Southern Rhodesia has been more a political threat to the United Kingdom than similar hostility in the United Nations. British Governments fear no consequences from frustrating the United Nations on Southern Rhodesia, but they risk their leadership of the Commonwealth and even the continued existence of

the Commonwealth if they cannot conciliate Commonwealth opposition over Southern Rhodesia. Both the United
Nations and the Commonwealth were potential allies of the
nationalists because of the prevalence in both of anti-
colonial states.

The Commonwealth

The nationalists have made sure that Commonwealth
leaders have known their case. In September 1962 Chirimbani, the London representative of ZAPU, handed in a
petition to the Commonwealth Prime Ministers' Conference.
After this, however, the lobbying was conducted by those
at the top of the hierarchy. In May 1963 Nkomo and four
other ZAPU leaders wrote to Commonwealth leaders asking them for action if Britain were about to give Southern
Rhodesia independence without majority rule, or if the
Southern Rhodesian Government declared independence
unilaterally. After the split Sithole appealed to the Heads
of States within the Commonwealth to secure an emergency
meeting on Southern Rhodesian independence before the
end of the year. He claimed to have received several favour-
able replies. For the meeting of the Commonwealth Heads
of States in July 1964 PCC/ZAPU sent three leaders from
Lusaka to lobby in London. Nyandoro headed the unofficial
delegation which was made up by Silundika and Moyo.
They worked hard and saw all the Heads of States, circulating to them a document containing a closely reasoned
argument that the franchise of the 1961 Constitution would
not give the Africans political control for fifty years.
ZANU sent a telegram to the British Prime Minister,
Douglas-Home, and copies of it to seven other Heads of
States. The Conference attempted to make the British Government promise to hold a constitutional conference on

45

Southern Rhodesia, but it escaped with a vague statement which committed it to nothing. At the next Commonwealth Conference of Heads of States in June 1965 Nyandoro was again back in London, urging the delegates to take a firm stand on Rhodesia and supporting his case with a duplicated memorandum. A ZANU delegation lobbied the Heads of States throughout the Conference and presented two documents. The leader of the ZANU delegation, Mukono, was in touch with Chitepo, the party's National Chairman, who, as Director of Public Prosecutions in Tanzania, attended the Conference as part of that country's delegation. This time, with the issue of UDI even more inflammatory than in the previous two years, the Conference fought hard to commit the British Government to positive action on the Rhodesian Africans' behalf. The final statement, while less evasive than in 1964, was still indecisive and Nyerere on behalf of Tanzania dissociated himself from it. Wilson, like his Conservative predecessors, held the Commonwealth leaders at bay and maintained the British Government's right, or rather power, to decide the Rhodesian problem as and when it chose. At the 1966 Commonwealth Conference Nyandoro and Moyo returned to make ineffective requests to members of an ineffective body, now faced with the *fait accompli* of independent Rhodesia.

The United Nations

In trying to move the British Government the Southern Rhodesian nationalists found the United Nations as ineffective a weapon as the Commonwealth, although it fired more frequent shots. The nationalists' campaign at the United Nations started in 1962, although Nkomo had made a sortie to New York in 1960 as part of his attempt to alert world opinion to the situation in Southern Rhodesia. In February 1962 ZAPU decided to appeal to the United Nations and sent Nkomo and Takawira to lobby for support.

On 27 November 1961 the General Assembly had set up a Special Committee to speed the abolition of colonialism (the Committee of Seventeen, later of Twenty-four). On 23 February 1962, acting on the recommendation of its Fourth Committee (on Trusteeship), the General Assembly had asked the Special Committee to consider whether Southern Rhodesia was a non-self-governing territory. If it were established that Southern Rhodesia were a colony, then the United Kingdom would have the responsibility under Article 74 of the United Nations Charter 'to develop self-government, to take due account of the political aspirations of the peoples, and to assist them in the progressive development of their free political institutions'. The Committe of Seventeen would try to make Britain take this responsibility seriously.

When Nkomo and Takawira came to New York in February 1962 the Fourth Committee already had the Southern Rhodesian question under consideration, as it had on its agenda in December 1961 a draft resolution recommending the General Assembly to have the Committee of Seventeen decide if Southern Rhodesia was self-governing or not. Discussion and decision on the resolution had been postponed till February 1962. The ZAPU mission was sent to lobby for support among the Afro-Asian countries for the proposal that the Committee of Seventeen should discuss Southern Rhodesia. After the General Assembly had agreed to this Nkomo left New York, returning when he heard that the Committee of Seventeen would hear ZAPU's evidence. ZAPU submitted a memorandum to the Committee and reinforced it by a cable alleging that the situation in Southern Rhodesia was deteriorating daily. On 16 March

Nkomo and Washington Malianga appeared before the Committee. This was the first formal appearance of the Southern Rhodesian African nationalists at the United Nations. Malianga remained silent throughout the proceedings. Nkomo presented a highly inaccurate account of Southern Rhodesian history on which he was questioned and highly complimented by members of the Committee. Although formally the Committee was considering whether Southern Rhodesia was self-governing, Nkomo took the opportunity to ask the Committee to look at the wider question, which it was not reluctant to do.

At Nkomo's invitation Garfield Todd, the ex-Prime Minister who since his resignation in 1958 had moved rapidly towards the nationalists' position, addressed the Committee on ZAPU's behalf. The Committee sent a sub-committee on Southern Rhodesia to London which reported against the British Government. Predictably the Committee advised the General Assembly that Southern Rhodesia was not self-governing, that the United Kingdom should be urged to take immediate steps to expedite African emancipation, and that the Assembly should take action as a matter of urgency. In June 1962, when Nkomo was again in New York, the Assembly duly endorsed its Committee's recommendations and Britain, which always protested that the United Nations had no authority to pronounce on Southern Rhodesian affairs, ignored the resolution.

Britain's position was that the United Nations had no right to discuss Southern Rhodesia, because it was internally self-governing and the United Nations' right would have existed only if Southern Rhodesia had been non-self-governing. Britain alone had responsibility for the territory. Britain could not give information to the United Nations about Southern Rhodesia because, as an internally self-governing territory, it did not give this information to

Britain. The representatives of Britain at the United Nations talked of cooperation with the Committee and commended the progressive policies of Whitehead, but they shielded Southern Rhodesia from the criticisms of the United Nations. The British Government took the line that only the British Government had the right to do anything about Southern Rhodesia and it had chosen not to do so.

The Committee (now of Twenty-four) kept Southern Rhodesia on its agenda and another representative of ZAPU, M. Zvobgo, made a statement to it on 12 September 1962. He complained that the British Government had ignored the Assembly's resolution and recounted the latest iniquities of the Southern Rhodesian Government. He repeated the nationalists' demands and suggested what the United Nations should do.

At the beginning of October the General Assembly passed a resolution demanding the release of political detainees in Southern Rhodesia and the lifting of the ban on ZAPU. The Assembly also declared Southern Rhodesia a danger to the peace. The same month the Fourth Committee, which had set in motion the United Nations activities on Southern Rhodesia, itself considered the issue again and provided a further opportunity for the nationalists to present their case in person. Dumbutshena appeared first, presenting well ZAPU's case against Whitehead's recent banning of their party. Sithole then continued the arguments against the Southern Rhodesian Government, claiming that it had provoked recent African violence. He too argued cogently, describing the poverty of Africans in his country and explaining in his capacity as National Chairman of ZAPU what economic policies ZAPU would give effect to when it became the Government. Josiah Chinamano, who followed Sithole, unlike him was not a full-time politician high in the nationalist hierarchy, but the headmaster of Highfield

49

Community School. A group of Africans and Europeans had established this school in the Salisbury township of Highfield to meet some of the African demand for secondary education, which the Government schools did not satisfy. Chinamano told the Committee that he had decided to come to the United Nations to counteract the representation of the multi-racial group which the United Federal Party (UFP, the governing party in Southern Rhodesia and the Federation) was unofficially sending over. This group explained its views to the Committee soon after Chinamano had tried in advance to remove the ground from under its feet. It was followed by another opponent of the UFP, Nathan Shamuyarira, who, like Chinamano, was not in the inner councils of ZAPU, but Editor of the *Daily News*, the only African newspaper in Southern Rhodesia. Shamuyarira contested the arguments of the UFP group in his first confrontation with the Committee, which later saw him alongside the UFP group and the representatives of an African nationalist splinter group, Pan-African Socialist Union. Its leader, Paul Mushonga, who had been Treasurer in ANC and a member of the NDP delegation to Home in April 1960, had already seen the Committee by himself before the joint meeting. The final ZAPU spokesman before the Fourth Committee was again Dumbutshena, who twice gave evidence that Africans in Southern Rhodesia would not obtain a majority in parliament in fifteen years, as the UFP claimed would happen under the new Constitution. He claimed that the Government was providing insufficient education to enable enough Africans to qualify for the franchise.

October 1962, the month after ZAPU was banned and two months before the first election under the 1961 Constitution, saw the most intensive nationalist activity at the United Nations, but the nationalists, in spite of having little

50

tangible reward for their efforts, continued to appeal to the United Nations after this date. The United Nations did not lose interest in Southern Rhodesia whether prompted by the nationalists or not.

In March 1963 Nkomo himself returned to the United Nations, where he brought the Committee of Twenty-four up to date on events in Southern Rhodesia since the last statements by ZAPU before the Committee in the previous October. The more right wing Rhodesian Front had replaced Whitehead's UFP at the December election. Nkomo distributed to the Committee copies of the new Government's Preservation of Constitutional Government Bill, which made subversive activity abroad a crime punishable by penalties up to twenty years imprisonment. After he had appeared formally before the Committee, Nkomo spoke to U Thant, the Acting Secretary General, and to the Afro-Asian group. Just over a month later Sithole was lobbying at the United Nations, although he made no formal statements to either committee. In October 1963 representatives of the two new nationalist parties caused by the split in the movement appeared before the Fourth Committee. Mugabe for ZANU urged the Committee to seek a more effective way to bring pressure on the adamant British Government. A week later Silundika spoke to the Committee on behalf of PCC/ZAPU.

In 1963 the United Nations continued to act, or rather speak, through various of its organs in favour of policies on Southern Rhodesia which the nationalists supported. Most notably, in September Ghana raised the question at the Security Council of the proposed transfer of a strong army and air force to Southern Rhodesia on the dissolution of the Federation at the end of the year. Britain vetoed a resolution against this transfer.

The African nationalists of Southern Rhodesia again

played a direct role in United Nations deliberations on the territory when Nyandoro spoke on behalf of PCC/ZAPU to the Committee of Twenty-four in April 1964. He told the Committee that the situation in Southern Rhodesia had deteriorated since Nkomo had spoken to it in March 1963. Nyandoro attempted to play down the conflict between the two nationalist parties which had started in July 1963, and at the same time to make capital for his own party by denying that ZANU had any popular support. A few days later Sithole counter-attacked for ZANU, while trying to maintain a united front with PCC on policy. He sent a cable to the United Nations supporting Nyandoro's stand, but denying that PCC commanded the support of all Africans in Southern Rhodesia. Sithole explained that Nyandoro had been out of active politics for five years and was therefore out of touch—a harsh appreciation of the facts, as Nyandoro had been in prison for four years for his leadership of ANC. Immediately after Nyandoro, Garfield Todd addressed the Committee for PCC/ZAPU, which he had now joined.

The United Nations continued to be vociferous on the nationalists' behalf. While a UDI became more likely throughout 1964 and 1965, the United Nations was constantly trying by resolutions to forestall it, and after it happened in November 1965 they tried the same method to reverse it. The Committee of Twenty-four went on listening to the nationalists.

In September 1964 Shamuyarira, on his way to take up an academic position at Princeton and in flight from the Southern Rhodesian Government, which had just banned both nationalist parties, lobbied in New York. He returned in April 1965, accompanied by a fellow member of ZANU, Mutambirwa, to address the Committee of Twenty-four. The following month the Committee started the first of its tours to Africa. In Lusaka the rival nationalist parties gave separate testimonies to the Committee, Nyandoro appearing for ZAPU, and Mukono, Matuure and Ntini for ZANU. The ZAPU headquarters also submitted a memorandum calling for United Nations military intervention in support of the internal African forces under the command of Nkomo (who was, of course, still in restriction). Outside the formal meeting a ZAPU supporter threw an egg at the American delegate in the belief that he was the British delegate. A year later the Committee returned to Africa, when it saw Silundika, with two ZAPU supporters, Dube and Wakatama, in Dar-es-Salaam, followed as usual by a ZANU contingent, on this occasion two officials from the Dar-es-Salaam office, Chihota and Pasipanodya. Later in its tour the Committee stopped in Cairo, where it heard Mpongo, the ZAPU representative there.

With and without the prompting of the nationalists the United Nations investigated the Southern Rhodesian problem and passed resolutions on it which had little or no effect on the policies of the British and Rhodesian Governments. The United Nations proved ineffective, but the nationalists hoped that it could help them to achieve what they had by themselves failed to achieve. To what extent had they worked out how they could use the United Nations?

No doubt the nationalists were partly motivated by a rather vague hope that if they could arouse 'world opinion' through the United Nations the British Government would eventually give way to their demands. At first they were probably content to give the United Nations the facts as they saw them and the policies they desired, leaving it to those in New York to fashion the means to achieve their ends. Later they became more sophisticated, although perhaps not more practical. The question of precisely what the United Nations could do was specifically raised when Dumbutshena, after having made his first statement to the Fourth Committee, was answering questions from its members. When asked what the United Nations should do, he was very vague. On the other hand, he shunned easy optimism or facile solutions: he doubted if economic sanctions could be effectively imposed, and he opposed any United Nations resolution which could not be enforced, as this would harm the Africans. One positive suggestion he made was that the United Nations should warn the British Government that the election proposed under the 1961 Constitution might lead to bloodshed. But this half-veiled threat of violence had not acted earlier as a goad to the British Government. However, other nationalists had hopes that they could move the United Nations to intervention in Southern Rhodesia if violence was occurring or was likely to occur. Sithole in October 1962 and Nkomo in March 1963 claimed that the desperation of Southern Rhodesian Africans might endanger world peace, although they did not explain precisely how. Mukono in 1965 suggested that Articles 39-42 of the Charter, which authorize the Security Council to act if peace is threatened, should be invoked before it was too late.

The nationalists sometimes proposed courses of action which the Committee of Twenty-four itself might take. Nkomo in 1963 suggested that it should send two or three of its members to try to persuade the British Government to do as the United Nations wished. Silundika in 1966 called for the expulsion of Britain from the Committee.

Shamuyarira in his statement before the Fourth Committee made the original suggestion that the Southern Rhodesian case might be taken before the International Court of Justice. The Indonesian delegate pointed out that if the United Nations handed over the question of Southern

Rhodesia to the International Court it could no longer deal with it itself. Nothing came of Shamuyarira's idea.

Pan-African institutions

The Southern Rhodesian nationalists decided to work through the Commonwealth and the United Nations as a result of their failure to secure their aims by directly confronting the British Government: their association with Pan-Africanism began before they approached the British Government. The first active participation came in December 1958 when ANC sent Nkomo, Nyandoro and Mushonga to Accra for the first All African Peoples' Conference. Here Nkomo met many other African nationalist leaders, a few governing independent states, most, like him, still struggling for power. From this time Nkomo and his fellow nationalists maintained and extended the contacts made at Accra by visiting particular African countries and by attending more Pan-African conferences. They continued to play a part in the All African Peoples' Conferences. Nkomo was a member of the Steering Committee which organized the Conferences. In January 1960 he attended the second Conference in Tunis and in March 1961 he led a nine man delegation to the third Conference in Cairo. Silundika led a small party to the fourth Conference in Accra in April 1962, although Whitehead's Government refused to give passports to four other members of ZAPU who planned to go.

Potentially more important to the Southern Rhodesian nationalists than these conferences of African nationalist parties were the conferences where full membership was restricted to independent African states. To some of these the Southern Rhodesian nationalists sent observers. For example, Silundika was a member of the NDP delegation to the second Conference of Independent African States at Addis Ababa in June 1960, and six of the ZAPU executives were again at Addis Ababa in May 1963 to witness the inauguration of the Organization of African Unity. OAU re-united the Pan-African forces split since the rival Conferences in 1961 at Casablanca and Monrovia and absorbed the All African Peoples' Organization.

Nationalists from Southern Rhodesia frequently informed Pan-African conferences and their subsidiary committees of their grievances and requested help. Nkomo, for example, presented a petition to the meeting of Foreign Ministers of the independent African states at Monrovia in August 1959. Five years later, to take another example, Shamuyarira stopped on his way to the United States at Addis Ababa in order to leave a memorandum with OAU Foreign Ministers, who were meeting to discuss the Congo.

Many of the conferences passed resolutions supporting the nationalists' policies for Southern Rhodesia. Picking at random, one may quote the Addis Ababa Conference of June 1960, which demanded that the Constitution of Southern Rhodesia should be democratized by introducing the principal of one man, one vote. It is difficult to estimate the effectiveness of the Southern Rhodesian nationalists' lobbying by formal petitions and informal conversations, because the Pan-African conferences would naturally be sensitive to the Southern Rhodesian issue and inclined to pass resolutions about it without the presence or pressure of Africans from Southern Rhodesia. On one occasion a Pan-African organization reacted to Nkomo's involvement in Pan-African politics with a more original and constructive, although not more effective, tactic than the customary conference resolutions. In November 1961 the Secretary of the All African Peoples' Organization gave Nkomo a letter to take to the British Prime Minister, in which a Pan-

African voice added its support to NDP's demand for a constitutional conference.

The most positive reactions of a Pan-African organization to participation and pressure by Southern Rhodesian nationalists came from OAU, which gave firm advice to the movement it was aiding. At the Addis Ababa Conference in May 1963 the independent states refused to give ZAPU the financial help it requested until the executive, then in exile on the advice of Nkomo, returned home and resumed political activities there. Later in the year the Liberation Committee (Committee of Nine), set up by OAU to assist those African countries still under colonial control, was told to help ZAPU only when it was again in action on the home front (Shamuyarira, 1965, 178). By the time all the executive had returned to Southern Rhodesia ZAPU had split and OAU was faced with a new problem, two rival parties weakening their joint nationalist cause by mutual hatred. OAU constantly tried, without success, to re-unite PCC/ZAPU and ZANU, although in December 1963 the Liberation Committee recognized both. The first meeting of the Liberation Committee in 1964 urged reconciliation, but in June Chikerema led a PCC delegation which argued to the Liberation Committee that PCC alone should receive material and financial help from OAU. The Committee did give PCC the larger share (Shamuyarira 1965, 191), but the policy of OAU remained to bring the two factions together. At the full Conference in Cairo in July 1964 OAU again declared its policy of ending the split, which it tried to carry into effect the following month. A reconciliation meeting was held in Lusaka, but it achieved nothing, because PCC were adamant in their policy of refusing to admit that ZANU existed. They consistently took the attitude that the leaders of ZANU had no following and nationalist unity would be restored by the return of the few deviants to the party of the people. Consequently PCC sent no representatives to Lusaka in August 1964. ZANU alone sent a five man delegation where representatives of Malawi and Tanganyika assembled on behalf of OAU. ZANU, the weaker of the two parties, was prepared to negotiate with PCC/ZAPU for a common front, provided that Nkomo were not leader. In December 1964 ZANU sent a formal memorandum to OAU requesting help in re-creating a single Rhodesian party, but OAU could not do then or after what it had failed to do earlier at Lusaka. PCC/ZAPU said that it was prepared to defy the continent, the world and God over reconciliation with ZANU and it successfully did this. A further OAU sub-committee of six members met in Nairobi in August 1965 to re-unite the two parties, but it only confirmed the failure of its predecessor. OAU said that they would recognize a nationalist government-in-exile if Rhodesia declared independence unilaterally, but would not recognize either government-in-exile if two were set up by both parties. This did nothing to end the feud.

OAU did not forget the ultimate goals of Southern Rhodesian nationalism while trying to reform its methods and organization. The Cairo Conference in July 1964 appointed two OAU members, Algeria and Senegal, to present the Southern Rhodesian nationalists' case to the United Nations Secretary General. This showed a more self-confident approach than previous Pan-African organizations. OAU undertook still more positive assistance when the Liberation Committee in February 1965 promised to supply arms which both PCC/ZAPU and ZANU requested.

One other Pan-African movement besides OAU had special importance for Southern Rhodesian nationalism. PAFMECA (Pan-African Freedom Movement of Eastern and Central Africa), because of its regional interests, was especially concerned about Southern Rhodesia. The organization, founded in 1958, existed before OAU and foreshadowed it in militancy and organization. PAFMECA set up a Liberation Committee to help the Africans still under colonial rule. Like its OAU successor it was hampered by lack of money, but in 1962 PAFMECSA (now including Southern Africa) decided to concentrate that year on helping Kaunda's UNIP fight the General Election in Northern Rhodesia. In 1963 it set Southern Rhodesia as its next target, but when OAU came into being PAFMECSA, although nominally continuing, became a much less active movement. Southern Rhodesia was a member from the inception, when its representatives were invited to the Mwanza Conference in Tanganyika in 1958. Africans from Southern Rhodesia, although not important in PAFMECSA's counsels, attended the organization's meetings: for example, Nkomo was at the summit conference (of the heads of parties) in January 1961. Nkomo was on the executive committee and Mugabe on the secretariat. The tangible results for the nationalist movement in Southern Rhodesia of its participation in PAFMECSA are not easy to see. Certainly Nkomo and his colleagues received advice and help at various stages from members of PAFMECSA, particularly from TANU as the Government of Tanganyika and from UNIP, the leading nationalist party of Northern Rhodesia. However, it is difficult to identify the role of PAFMECSA in determining the behaviour of individual parties and politicians who were members of it. Northern Rhodesian and Nyasaland nationalists have had special relations with Southern Rhodesian nationalists which are independent of PAFMECSA.

Other international institutions

The Southern Rhodesian nationalists' association with Pan-

Africanism led them naturally to support and to seek support from the wider organizations to which Pan-Africanism was allied by interest and ideology. Representatives went to Afro-Asian Peoples' Solidarity Conferences. Silundika, for example, was at Bandung in April 1961, Alfred Gondo at Moshi, Tanganyika, in February 1963, and Chikerema and Joseph Msika in Cyprus in September 1964. In April 1960 Southern Rhodesia was on the directing committee which met at Conakry, The Afro-Asian Solidarity Organization gave the Southern Rhodesian nationalists financial help.

The conferences of neutralist states brought together many united in hatred of imperialism. Consequently the Southern Rhodesian nationalists sent along observers. Moton Malianga travelled to the first neutralist conference at Belgrade in 1961 on behalf of NDP, and Henry Hamadziripi represented ZANU at Cairo in 1964.

Attending these neutralist and Afro-Asian conferences the Southern Rhodesian nationalists met more powerful men than themselves with similar ideologies, from whom they received sympathy and encouragement. As at the Pan-African conferences, the United Nations and the Commonwealth Prime Ministers' Conferences, they found many vociferous allies whose help proved more moral than practical.

4

Links in Central Africa

The most frequent political contacts between Africans of Southern Rhodesia and Africans from other countries have been made with those from Northern Rhodesia and Nyasaland. Much migrant labour has come from the northern territories to Southern Rhodesia and there is a considerable movement from the south to Northern Rhodesia, especially to the mines of the Copperbelt. Consequently Africans from all three British Central African territories have mixed socially, most of all in the townships of Southern Rhodesia. As political consciousness grew, political interaction between nationalists from the different colonies increased.

African opposition to the Federation in the three territories

These growing connections were unintentionally fostered by the white minorities whose political representatives helped to impose the Federation of Rhodesia and Nyasaland on unwilling Africans. When federation was discussed in the late 1940's and early 1950's, Africans from all three territories protested, because they feared that the racially discriminatory policies of Southern Rhodesia, virtually independent of Britain in its internal affairs, might be foisted on Northern Rhodesia and Nyasaland. Here the position of the Africans was to some extent safeguarded because these colonies were goverened by administrations responsible to the Colonial Office in London. In 1951 representatives of African organizations from the three territories met at Fort Jameson and condemned the proposed federation. Members of the African Voice Association, the Reformed Industrial and Commercial Workers' Union and the African National Congress (the milder forebear of the militant 1957 Congress) represented Southern Rhodesian Africans. After the Fort Jameson conference the All-African Convention was formed in Southern Rhodesia to mobilize African opinion against federation, which nevertheless became a reality in 1953. The Convention, never an effective political body, crumbled away in 1954, but African suspicions of Federation were not removed by experience of its working. When the African National Congress was resuscitated in 1957 it attacked the Federation and this remained the policy of African nationalism in Southern Rhodesia until the Federation ended in December 1963. Africans from the northern territories had more to fear from Federation than those in Southern Rhodesia, who might even have hoped for some liberalization of their Government's racial policies under the influence of the Federation's averred ideology of multi-racial partnership. In fact, all the nationalist parties and their predecessors, like the Voice Association, remained uniformly hostile to Federation. Only a small number of Southern Rhodesian Africans at any time showed any faith in Federation. It received very little support from traditional leaders who met the Commonwealth Secretary, Gordon Walker, in 1951. A small number of mainly middle class Africans joined the predominantly European United Rhodesia Party, which supported Federation. But several Africans who joined, like the later ZANU leader, Shamuyarira, became disillusioned and joined the national-

62

ists. Federation failed to provide a politically integrated Central Africa, but ironically it acted as a symbol of European domination which united Africans in the three territories. Being in the Federation and wanting to be out of it created a stronger feeling of common purpose among politically conscious Africans in Central Africa than if they had merely shared a common language in English and a common wish to end their social subordination by gaining political control.

Association with the African National Congresses of Northern Rhodesia and Nyasaland 1956-1959

The nationalist Congresses of Northern Rhodesia and Nyasaland were effectively organized movements with wide support before nationalism in Southern Rhodesia had developed beyond sporadic local outbursts. The Nyasaland Congress in particular had a long record of activism. It provided practical lessons in militancy to the less politically mature Africans of Southern Rhodesia. Nor were the northern Congresses merely distant examples, for the African parties from the two northern territories had branches in Southern Rhodesia amongst the migrant workers. When the Youth League was founded in 1956, marking the beginning of radical organized nationalism in Southern Rhodesia, the indigenous leaders received help from northern nationalists. Nyasas influence on Southern Rhodesian African politics, which started in the 1920's, was particularly important in the crucial year of 1956. Dunduza Chisiza, who in 1958 was to be one of the most dynamic leaders of the Nyasaland African National Congress and largely responsible, along with Chipembere and Chiume, for exciting his countrymen into heated protest against the colonial administration, lived in 1956 in Salisbury and was a friend of

Nyandoro and Chikerema. Together they started the Youth League which formed the nucleus a year later of the revived Congress. Another Nyasa politician, Wellington Chirwa, a Federal M.P. who constantly attacked the Federation, was also associated with the Youth League in its early days. At the first open meeting of the Youth League in May 1956 a prominent Northern Rhodesian nationalist, Dauti Yamba, who was, like Chirwa, an anti-Federation Federal M.P., was one of the speakers (as he was at the first meeting of the new ANC in 1957). In July 1956 the Southern Rhodesian Government expelled Chisiza, another Nyasaland African and a Northern Rhodesian African from Southern Rhodesia. While hindering in a small way the active collaboration between African politicians from the three territories this action contributed to the feeling of solidarity between Africans from both Rhodesia and Nyasaland. The Youth League protested against the deportation at a mass meeting and even moderate, non-nationalist Africans in the URP and the Interracial Society declared themselves against the Government's action. This exclusion of northern nationalists from Southern Rhodesia underlined for the nationalists the hollowness of the Federation.

Two years later, by which time the Southern Rhodesian ANC was flourishing, nationalists from all the constituent parts of the Federation made deliberate moves to coordinate their activities. In December 1957 leaders of the Congresses from the three colonies met for a conference at Lusaka, where they discussed tactics and planned future conferences. When Dr. Hastings Banda returned to Africa to become the messianic leader of the Nyasaland African National Congress, he spoke in Salisbury (December 1958) and was rapturously received. A meeting of the Secretaries General of the four Congresses (Northern Rhodesia had two rival Congresses under Nkumbula and Kaunda) was arranged for January 1959 in Salisbury to plan a summit conference in Blantyre the following month, but the delegates from the Zambia and the Nyasaland African National Congresses were forbidden to enter the country. Nyandoro, representing Southern Rhodesia, travelled to Blantyre to meet representatives from the northern territories, but Sipalo, from the Zambia ANC, had been banned from Nyasaland. Finally a meeting of spokesmen from the four Congresses was held in Lusaka. The proposed summit conference did not take place because all the Congresses except Nkumbula's were banned by their respective territorial governments. Had it met the conference would have discussed how the Congresses could concert common action. In the same month as his visit to Lusaka as Secretary General of the Southern Rhodesian ANC Nyandoro attended the famous meeting of the Nyasaland ANC in the bush near Blantyre at which it was decided to conduct in Nyasaland an 'all-out campaign to defy the Government, violence not excluded' (Devlin Report, 1959, 51). Because the Government believed that this meeting had plotted a massacre, it banned the Nyasaland ANC and arrested its leaders.

When the Southern Rhodesian Government banned the Southern Rhodesian Congress in February 1959 it levelled against it the charge that it had cooperated with the other Congresses of the Federation. The Beadle Commission investigating this charge along with others concluded from evidence they collected that the Southern Rhodesian ANC had collaborated with the Nyasaland ANC and the Zambia ANC, which in the opinion of the Commission were 'subversive organizations committed to a policy of violence' (Beadle Report, 1959, 18-19). How far the Southern Rhodesian Congress was implicated in any violence and subversion of the other Congresses the Beadle Report fails

65

to establish. The three banned Congresses were united by the friendly relations of their leaders, by their intentions, apparently unrealized, to coordinate their political actions (the Blantyre summit conference was never held) and by their common purposes and principles. The extent to which the leaders of the northern Congresses influenced or stimulated Nyandoro and his colleagues is difficult to estimate. There is a danger of attributing too much to the more developed nationalist movements of the north. The nationalist movement in Southern Rhodesia had a record since 1956 of sustained militancy which cannot be attributed in any large degree to outside influence. The Beadle Report itself provided evidence of the Southern Rhodesian Congress leaders' self-generated radicalism. The attack in the rural areas on the Native Land Husbandry Act, for example, was particular to Southern Rhodesia. Furthermore, Nyandoro and Chikerema, unlike Nkomo in later years, spent a very small proportion of their time talking outside the country, a very large part rousing political consciousness within it. Nyandoro by his presence at the Blantyre bush meeting was probably merely a witness of the decision of the Nyasaland Congress, of which he was not a member, although his inflammatory speeches in his own country suggest he would have sympathized with the advocacy of violent policies. But this does not prove that he or his movement was directed or even given detailed advice by the Nyasa leaders, nor that he played a part in determining their policy.

One can only speculate whether the Congresses of the Federation would have synchronized political action, violent or passive, if the bans had not prevented the Blantyre conference. The association of the leaders of the various Congresses in the year preceding the bans may have increased the enthusiasm of their followers. When the Governments of the three territories banned the Congresses they may have boosted the nationalists' sense of solidarity as much as the Congresses' own efforts at cooperation did.

Nationalist collaboration during the review of the Federation, 1960

In 1960 the Monckton Commission visited Central Africa to examine the working of the Federation. The nationalist parties which had been banned were now re-formed and all refused to give evidence to the Commission, because it could not, according to its terms of reference, recommend the dissolution of the Federation which the nationalists demanded. The British Government arranged a conference in London at the end of 1960 to review the Federation in the light of the Monckton Commission's findings. Kaunda and Banda, nationalist leaders from the northern territories, were invited to the conference. Nkomo and his colleagues from NDP arrived in London without having been invited by the Southern Rhodesian Prime Minister to the Federal Review Conference. At the last moment Whitehead agreed to NDP's presence at the Federal Review Conference and consented to participate in a conference on Southern Rhodesia itself. The British Government may have pressed Whitehead to allow NDP at the conference table because its absence threatened to cause a boycott by nationalists from the other two territories. Before and during this round of conferences Nkomo and the NDP delegation liaised with the African representatives of Northern Rhodesia and Nyasaland. The Conference on the hated Federation created the occasion for protracted collaboration between the nationalist leaders.

All the nationalist leaders demonstrated their hostility to the Federal Review Conference. Nkomo and Kaunda made it clear that their main purpose in coming to London

67

was to press for constitutional advances at territorial conferences, and Banda supported them. The three leaders had talks in London before the Federal Review Conference to decide their attitude towards it. They then announced that their concerted policy was to attend the Conference provided that it did not hold up the territorial conferences. Early in the Federal Review Conference Banda walked out, apparently to the surprise of Kaunda and Nkomo, who remained. At the next session, however, the Northern Rhodesian and Southern Rhodesian nationalists, not to be outshone by Banda, also walked out. Two days later Banda, Kaunda and Nkomo had another meeting, but the Federal Review Conference was virtually dead and the energies of Nkomo and Kaunda were soon concentrated on the problems of the separate territorial conferences.

Advice and censure from the northern nationalists, 1961 onwards

The Southern Rhodesian Conference proved abortive in London, but was eventually held in February 1961 in Salisbury. The agreement of Nkomo at the Conference to constitutional proposals which fell far short of one man, one vote, brought criticism from N. Mundia, acting Secretary General of UNIP, the successor to the Zambia ANC. UNIP wanted no weakness in the stand of their allies south of the Zambesi, when they themselves were bargaining hard with the British Government for a more democratic constitution for Northern Rhodesia. Nkomo soon repudiated the constitutional agreement, but the contribution of the Northern Rhodesians to his change of mind was much smaller than that of Nkomo's own lieutenants in NDP. Later in the year Banda derided the 'spineless leaders' in Southern Rhodesia, although NDP had retracted its acceptance of the constitutional proposals. Although in October Banda and Nkomo became reconciled, 1961 marked the beginning of an era when the nationalists of Northern Rhodesia and Nyasaland took it upon themselves to advise their allies in the south, often with at least a note of censure. In 1961 Kaunda was negotiating and Banda had secured major constitutional advances from Britain and they continued to press hard for complete self-government, which they obtained in 1964. They accelerated away from the nationalists of Southern Rhodesia, who started later and met more determined opposition. Conscious of their roles as elder brothers in the nationalist family of Central Africa the northern nationalists both encouraged and chided those from the south. This is illustrated by statements by UNIP leaders at the banning of ZAPU, and by the attitudes of Kaunda and Banda to the rivalry between PCC and ZANU.

When the Southern Rhodesian Government banned ZAPU in September 1962 Nkomo was in Lusaka, having stopped there on his way back to Salisbury from Dar-es-Salaam to have talks with Kaunda. Since the Federal Review Conference the two leaders had met several times. In May 1962 they had appeared together at a rally in Lusaka. At the September talks Kaunda promised to give ZAPU financial aid after he had won power in the October election, and to put pressure on the British Government to alter the Southern Rhodesian Constitution. The day after the talks ZAPU was banned and Nkomo, who was due to return home, cancelled his flight. He announced that he would spend a few days conferring with party branches in Northern Rhodesia before going back to expected arrest. However, acting on information which later proved false that two of his lieutenants had been put in gaol and maltreated, he changed plans at the last moment and without announcement drove to Tanganyika. After a week in which he twice consulted Kawawa, the Tanganyikan Prime Minister, Nkomo finally did return home. After Nkomo's flight to Tanganyika Kaunda said that the ZAPU leader was wise because there was a plot against his life. However, some members of ZAPU believed that Kaunda, in spite of his public support of Nkomo, had privately urged him to return to Salisbury. Other UNIP leaders criticized Nkomo's conduct. While he was still delaying in Lusaka, Arthur Wina attacked Nkomo for indecision and strongly advised him that his political leadership and a solution to the Southern Rhodesian crisis depended on his presence in Southern Rhodesia. Sikota Wina also recommended Nkomo to return and Mainza Chona thought that his secret flight would have a bad effect on the Southern Rhodesian Africans. The opinions of the UNIP leaders may have contributed to Nkomo's eventual decision to return.

Between the expression of these opinions and the strong reactions by the Northern Rhodesian and Nyasaland nationalists to the division in the Southern Rhodesian movement in July 1963, the main contact between northern and southern nationalists was a further series of talks between Nkomo and Kaunda, who from November 1962 was a Minister. In January 1963 they had discussions over a period of two days, at the end of which they issued a joint statement condemning the Federation and insisting that the ban on ZAPU must be lifted. In March 1963 Nkomo talked to Kaunda in Lusaka about the UNIP leader's forthcoming meeting in London with R. A. Butler about the future of the Federation, now virtually doomed. Although not invited to these talks because he did not head a government, Nkomo went to London where he again conferred with Kaunda. In June 1963 the two nationalist leaders again exchanged views, this time discussing future economic links between Northern and Southern Rhodesia. By these meetings Nkomo preserved at least the appearance of solidarity between the nationalist movements of the two Rhodesias, each pushing towards self-government but with greatly different speeds and success. From this alliance Nkomo hoped to gain moral reinforcement.

The episode in Southern Rhodesian nationalist history which stimulated the most determined and prolonged attempts by northern nationalists to supervise policies in the south was the conflict between pro- and anti-Nkomo factions after July 1963. The northern leaders realized that the Southern Rhodesian nationalist movement, already struggling under severe difficulties, would be seriously weakened as a fighting force against white minority rule if it was divided into two hostile factions, especially when war between them was more than metaphorical. Both Kaunda and Banda, who was now Prime Minister, strongly urged PCC/ZAPU and ZANU to resolve their differences and re-unite. In April 1964, for example, Banda spoke in favour of a government-in-exile in the event of a UDI and said that he hoped to see all the Southern Rhodesian nationalists united in this government. Sithole's reply in which he refused to collaborate with Nkomo was typical of the Southern Rhodesian Africans' refusal to heed the appeals for compromise which came from the north.

Demanding unity among Southern Rhodesian nationalists did not prevent UNIP and Banda's Malawi Congress Party from taking sides in the civil war south of the Zambesi. Very soon after the split in July 1963 two of Nkomo's principal opponents, Takawira and Washington Malianga, visited Blantyre and saw officials of the Malawi Congress Party. When the new parties were formed in August Banda came out for Sithole, whom he thought 'more able, honest and sincere' than Nkomo. Banda claimed that Nkomo had let him down in 1952 by attending a conference to discuss federation after saying he would not. Also, Banda perhaps still blamed Nkomo for initially accepting the 1961 constitutional proposals, although Sithole, who in 1963 criticized Nkomo as a leader, was also an NDP delegate to the constitutional Conference of 1961 which agreed to the proposals. Although trying to rebuild a united front in Southern Rhodesia Banda shared Sithole's mistrust of Nkomo's leadership, which was the sole ostensible cause of the split. In March and June 1964 Sithole went to Nyasaland for talks with Banda at Banda's invitation. In July Banda invited ZANU but not ZAPU to the Malawi independence celebrations.

Kaunda was much slower to commit himself in the Southern Rhodesian dispute, presumably hoping that a re-unification of the adversaries would obviate the need to support either party. However, in April 1964 Kaunda announced his support of Nkomo. The prospect of a reconciliation seemed remote, so Kaunda decided he should back the party which appeared clearly to him to have the greater mass following. UNIP consequently became a champion of ZAPU while remaining critical of all Southern Rhodesian nationalists for their hostility to each other. One overt sign of Kaunda's support for ZAPU occurred in June 1964 when Chikerema spoke on behalf of ZAPU at a UNIP rally in Lusaka.

The participation of the Northern Rhodesian and Nyasa-land leaders in the Southern Rhodesian dispute produced violence and vituperation between the nationalists of the three Central African countries. ZAPU and ZANU spokesmen savaged the leaders of the northern territories in print. Edson Sithole on behalf of ZANU wrote an article in the Salisbury *Daily News* of 25 April 1964 which alleged that Kaunda's support of Nkomo was unwarranted interference in Southern Rhodesian African politics and based on ignorance of the facts involved. In the 20 June 1964 issue of *Zimbabwe Sun*, a PCC organ published in Salisbury, an article assaulted Banda vigorously for supporting ZANU. More serious than these verbal missiles was the physical violence which broke out between rival parties from different countries. In mid-1964 members of the UNIP Youth League attacked ZANU offices in Lusaka, Ndola and Kitwe, events joyfully recounted in PCC's *Zimbabwe Sun*. In Southern Rhodesia members of PCC assaulted Africans from Malawi, most of whom had been long and peacefully resident in Southern Rhodesia. Although disowned by Nkomo, some PCC followers revenged themselves on Banda by persecuting his countrymen. Similarly ZANU members avenged Kaunda's support for their enemy by attacking UNIP members who lived in Southern Rhodesia. The split in the Southern Rhodesian nationalist movement not only made enemies of previous allies amongst Southern Rhodesian Africans, but also embittered relations between nationalists with similar ideals from different territories.

However, supporting one of the competing Southern Rhodesian parties did not lead either Kaunda or Banda to forbid the activities of the party he opposed in his territory. But each deported an official of the party with which he did not sympathize and this was interpreted by the offended party in each case as an act of hostility. In June 1964 Kaunda expelled Stanley Parirewa, the ZANU organizer in Northern Rhodesia, ostensibly at least on the grounds that he had worked and engaged in political activity in Northern Rhodesia without seeking formal permission from the Northern Rhodesian authorities to live or work in the country. The following month Banda's Government deported a ZAPU official.

The toleration by Kaunda's Government of the Rhodesian nationalists, in spite of their division, the enmities it engendered, and their persisting impotence, became increasingly important to both PCC/ZAPU and ZANU as their organization of guerilla warfare from Lusaka developed. Occasionally those transporting weapons through Zambia were charged by the police with illegal possession of arms. The Zambian Government, however, did not prevent either Rhodesian nationalist party from using Lusaka as a centre from which to send men abroad for military training, and after this training to Rhodesia as guerillas, even when hundreds of these trained men were known to be living in Zambia.

Although tolerating the Rhodesian nationalists and their activities UNIP occasionally expressed public impatience with them. Sikota Wina complained in February 1964 about their 'childish squabbling'. In November 1965 Kaunda untypically exploded, at a rally at Broken Hill, in denunciation of the Rhodesian nationalist leaders who lived out of Rhodesia, talked much and achieved so little even after the provocation of UDI. He condemned their shouting for the indiscriminate killing of Rhodesian whites from the comfort of exile. 'I have grown tired of talking to these gentlemen who are so fond of chicken in the basket [a Lusaka hotel delicacy]. . . . You call them nationalists. I call them stupid idiots.'

5
Headquarters abroad

London, 1959-1961

One response by the Southern Rhodesian nationalists to the
Government's hindering their activities at home has been
to establish headquarters abroad. Nkomo set the prece-
dent in 1959 when he made London the centre of his overseas activities after ANC had been banned. While the
nationalist movement had no open, legal form in Southern
Rhodesia, Nkomo and his London headquarters served as
symbols of the continuing struggle. They were a visible link
between ANC and the new party, NDP, formed in January
1960. Now in charge of NDP's overseas headquarters,
Nkomo continued to operate from London until November
of that year. This was no longer an alternative to a headquarters in Southern Rhodesia, but a joint spearhead with
it. The London headquarters also provided Nkomo with
a safe and potentially productive job at a time when he
risked detention if he returned to Southern Rhodesia. Many
leaders had been released by 1960, but several of the most
important remained in the Government's hands. After
Nkomo did finally return home in November 1960, Takawira came to London to take charge of NDP's overseas
headquarters. Unlike Nkomo he was not a fugitive from

Southern Rhodesia. When Takawira left London at the formation of ZAPU, an overseas headquarters ceased to exist, although Takawira continued to direct activities abroad, now exercising his command from Southern Rhodesia.

Dar-es-Salaam, 1962-1963

When NDP was banned in December 1961 the party immediately reconstituted itself in a legally defensible form as ZAPU, but when ZAPU was in turn outlawed the following September the executive had already agreed (in July) not to form another party, but to operate underground. As Nkomo had experienced exile from 1958 to 1960 and had run a headquarters abroad, it was not perhaps surprising that he favoured establishing a headquarters, this time in Dar-es-Salaam, if ZAPU were banned. The plan was to move the national executive, and thus the organizational head of the movement, out of Southern Rhodesia. This, of course, was a new policy. Probably when Nkomo was in New York in June 1962 some United Nations representatives urged him to form a government-in-exile if his party were proscribed. On the other hand it seems that Dr T. S. Parirenyatwa, Deputy President of ZAPU till his death in August 1962, was opposed to setting up an exile organization in Dar-es-Salaam and was travelling to dissuade Nkomo from this plan when he was killed in a road accident. By the beginning of September the leaders of ZAPU were expecting the Government to strike soon at their party. In the first week of the month Nkomo suddenly flew to Tanganyika. It appears that some of the national executive did not know the purpose of his visit. Mugabe, who was in charge of publicity, made no announcement and, when asked, refused to say why Nkomo had gone. He said that the national executive had decided that it was urgent for Nkomo to visit Dar-es-Salaam, where he would see the Prime Minister, Kawawa. Mugabe, who was vague about how long Nkomo would be away, may have been deliberately secretive about the reason for Nkomo's flight, or he may have been ignorant of it and trying to disguise this. In Dar-es-Salaam Nkomo made a statement that the Southern Rhodesian Government had been plotting to kill him, having ordered the police to provoke trouble at Nkomo's meetings and to shoot him while pacifying the disturbance. Presumably by this highly coloured story Nkomo may have been providing an explanation for his absence and/or a partial justification for any exile he might choose for himself in the future. The African *Daily News* in Salisbury thought Nkomo was in Dar-es-Salaam in connection with plans to form a government-in-exile if ZAPU should be banned. They believed ZAPU funds had been directed to Dar-es-Salaam, so that the Southern Rhodesian Government could not confiscate all ZAPU's assets if it banned the party. *The Times* correspondent in Salisbury said it was understood that while Kawawa supported a government-in-exile Nyerere was more cautious.

The Southern Rhodesian Government duly banned ZAPU on 20 September 1962. Nkomo was still out of the country and by now in Lusaka. On 22 September Nkomo, who had postponed his return to Salisbury after hearing of the Government's move against ZAPU, held a press conference, where he announced that an emergency organization would be set up in Dar-es-Salaam. Nkomo had appointed nine of his colleagues to live outside Southern Rhodesia, four to strengthen ZAPU offices in Cairo, Ghana, London and New York, four to work under Sithole in Dar-es-Salaam. Party branches in Northern Rhodesia and Nyasaland would be coordinated with the officials in Dar-es-Salaam to free Southern Rhodesia. Nkomo expressed the intention to return himself almost immediately to Southern Rhodesia, but in fact he mysteriously disappeared from Lusaka and reappeared in Tanganyika. It seems that just before he was due to return to Salisbury Nkomo was informed by Msika, a junior member of the ZAPU executive, that Mugabe and Takawira, two leaders arrested by the Government, had not merely been restricted to their tribal areas, as at first thought, but had been put in gaol and badly treated. This information, which later proved to be false, seems to have stopped Nkomo from returning to Salisbury. According to Nkomo himself, he left Lusaka because there was a plot to murder him in Northern Rhodesia and went to Dar-es-Salaam to meet two members of the ZAPU executive. Once there Nkomo denied that he intended to set up a government-in-exile in Dar-es-Salaam, as some journalists had suggested, and described the organization there as the party executive's temporary headquarters. He twice had talks with Kawawa, who offered ZAPU facilities for this overseas committee, and also consulted his ZAPU colleagues in Dar-es-Salaam, Sithole and A. Mukhahlera. They agreed with the plan for a headquarters in Dar-es-Salaam and Sithole urged Nkomo to go home. Although on arriving in Dar-es-Salaam Nkomo had spoken of visiting London and New York, he announced on 28 September that he would return to Salisbury four days later, which this time he did.

Nkomo definitely stated after the banning of ZAPU that Sithole was to lead the ZAPU organization in Dar-es-Salaam, but, while Nkomo himself remained outside Southern Rhodesia, the possibility must have existed that he, as President of ZAPU, would be in charge of the overseas headquarters. He seems to have shown a penchant during September 1962 for activity outside Southern Rhodesia. However, after Nkomo had been persuaded to return home, it was Sithole who ran the headquarters in Dar-es-Salaam. It is difficult to discover how far Nkomo's plan materialized for nine ZAPU leaders, including the coordinating group in Dar-es-Salaam, to work abroad. Sithole himself did make Dar-es-Salaam his base. When Nkomo flew back to Salisbury in October 1962, Sithole accompanied him as far as Nairobi and then travelled on via London to New York to represent ZAPU at the United Nations. In December he sent a letter from Dar-es-Salaam to all Africans eligible to vote urging them not to vote in the first General Election under the 1961 Constitution. While leading ZAPU abroad, Sithole also broadcast from Dar-es-Salaam to Africans in Southern Rhodesia, and wrote a pamphlet putting ZAPU's case, for circulation through ZAPU's external offices.

Between September and December 1962, when several ZAPU leaders, including Nkomo, were restricted and under police supervision, Nkomo managed to hold a meeting of the executive. According to Shamuyarira (1965, 175), who later opposed Nkomo, Nkomo suggested at this meeting that the ZAPU executive should flee to Dar-es-Salaam via Bechuanaland and set up a government-in-exile. This proposal was, says Shamuyarira, 'turned down flatly by the rest of the executive'.

In the new year the possibility of establishing a government-in-exile became an acknowledged policy of ZAPU, but only in a certain contingency. The Rhodesian Front, elected to form a government in December 1962, soon began to negotiate with the British Government for independence, and some elements in the party spoke of the possibility of a unilateral declaration of independence if Southern Rhodesia could not obtain independence on satisfactory terms from Britain. ZAPU's response was the declaration of their intent to set up a government-in-exile if the

79

Southern Rhodesian Government declared independence illegally.

The new Prime Minister, Winston Field, as well as trying to obtain independence, also said that he could destroy the nationalist movement by detaining about three hundred Africans. Nkomo probably felt that the dangers of a right wing Government becoming independent and paralysing the nationalist movement made it more than ever necessary to put the national executive beyond the reach of the Government outside Southern Rhodesia. There it could form a government-in-exile if the need arose.

After his release from restriction (in January 1963) Nkomo resumed his efforts to make Dar-es-Salaam a strong centre of ZAPU activities. Early in February two members of the executive, Washington Malianga and J. Z. Moyo, were sent to Dar-es-Salaam to talk to those already there. In the middle of March Nkomo and Chikerema (a member of the ZAPU executive who was released in January 1963 after four years in prison for his pioneer role in ANC) travelled to Tunduma in Southern Tanganyika to meet Sithole. In Dar-es-Salaam they found that he had left for Egypt at the end of January and had not returned. Nkomo and Chikerema went on to London to see R. A. Butler about the talks he was to have with Field. Here they learnt from Dumbutshena that Sithole had been in London for a week but had now left. Nkomo then moved on to the United Nations and while in New York met Msika and Miss Ngwenya, two junior members of the ZAPU executive who were on visits there. He got their agreement to actions ZAPU intended to take as a result of Field's attempts to get independence. In his account of this discussion Nkomo does not say what the actions were, but events which followed soon after suggest that they included the move of the national executive from Southern Rhodesia. On returning to London Nkomo finally did meet Sithole, who, according to Nkomo, agreed with action (again unspecified in Nkomo's account) which was proposed. Nkomo says that he asked Sithole to come to Dar-es-Salaam to complete arrangements and to get a full report of his activities. Sithole replied that he would join Nkomo later in Dar-es-Salaam, as he had some appointments in London. Before returning to Southern Rhodesia Nkomo spent three days in Dar-es-Salaam, but Sithole did not come during that time. While Nkomo was in Dar-es-Salaam Chikerema joined him and they discussed with the ZAPU people there the plan of action. At the end of March Nkomo returned to Salisbury. In just under a fortnight the ZAPU national executive decided to leave for Tanganyika. Chikerema alone would stay a little longer. A meeting of the executive took place in Bulawayo, where Nkomo was able to persuade the others of the wisdom of this plan, because, according to Shamuyarira, Nkomo could tell them that this was the wish of Pan-African leaders, whom only he had recently met.

Those on the executive who were in the country left Southern Rhodesia individually in early April. Two, Mugabe and Takawira, were breaking the conditions of bail by leaving. Mugabe was doubtful whether this policy was the right one. Of those executive members already abroad Msika and Miss Ngwenya arrived in Dar-es-Salaam from the United States and Mukhahlera from Asia. Cables were sent to London and New York asking Sithole to join the others in Dar-es-Salaam, but they failed to reach him. Ten leaders were now assembled in Dar-es-Salaam, the whole executive except Sithole, Chikerema, who stayed in Southern Rhodesia by design, and one other (possibly Ncube who later in the year was out of politics and in full-time employment). These ten allocated duties to each other. Somewhat surprisingly Nkomo said later that 'one of the

81

F

important duties of our plan was that after a certain stage, I and a certain number of my colleagues had to return home'. It was agreed that this would be after the Addis Ababa Pan-African Conference. Shamuyarira comments on the vagueness of this and suggests that one reason for going home again was the shortage of money and accommodation in Dar-es-Salaam for the leaders and their wives. Also, according to Shamuyarira, the members of the executive were astounded to find when they arrived in Dar-es-Salaam that Nyerere, the President of Tanganyika, had not sanctioned the move and was indeed surprised to find them there. To the press Nkomo announced that he and his colleagues were not forming a government-in-exile in Dar-es-Salaam, but were there 'to intensify and re-direct our efforts, to achieve our goal through vigorous and positive action'.

Nkomo and Takawira departed for visits to various African countries and in May Nkomo, Sithole, Takawira, J. Z. Moyo, Washington Malianga and Mugabe attended the Addis Ababa Conference. According to Nkomo, the Foreign Ministers and Heads of State of the independent African countries received the Southern Rhodesian case well. Shamuyarira denies Nkomo's story, and maintains that the states refused financial aid to ZAPU until the leaders were active at home. Ghana and Algeria, Shamuyarira asserts, 'were particularly critical of the exodus, and of the lack of action inside Southern Rhodesia'.

At Addis Ababa the executive had a brief meeting. Shamuyarira says that it discussed the leadership and was inconclusive. Sithole, who had arrived on the plane of the Congolese Prime Minister, Adoula, had to leave with him for Leopoldville before anything definite had been decided. It was agreed that the matter would be discussed at a meeting after reaching Dar-es-Salaam. Nkomo maintains that there was no sign of dissatisfaction among the six leaders at the Addis Ababa Conference.

After the Conference Nkomo asked Sithole to return from the Congo within five days. Takawira was sent by Nkomo with a letter to Butler in London, with instructions to return as quickly as possible. Moyo went off to Ghana, while the other Addis Ababa delegates, Nkomo, Mugabe and Malianga, returned to Dar-es-Salaam. Nkomo relates that he waited a fortnight in Dar-es-Salaam for Sithole and Takawira to return and cabled to them without success (the ZANU story is that Nkomo deliberately dispersed the executive to prevent a new discussion of the leadership). After these two weeks Nkomo decided to return to Southern Rhodesia. Shamuyarira claims that Nyerere told Nkomo that it was time he went back, as the leaders at Addis Ababa had suggested. Nkomo says that his decision was prompted by the announcement of the Conference at Victoria Falls on the dismantling of the Federation, and by Field's having failed to negotiate independence for Southern Rhodesia. It is not easy to see why the Conference about the Federation should have prompted Nkomo to return to Southern Rhodesia. In fact, while it was on he appeared on the Northern Rhodesian side of the Victoria Falls in Livingstone. Field's failure to obtain independence may have provided a reason for Nkomo's return, as there was no immediate prospect of independence and therefore no need for Nkomo to be ready to form a government-in-exile. But, if Nkomo was to return, why not the others? It is possible that Nkomo was returning partly at least in accordance with the plan he vaguely describes, which was, according to him, made soon after the flight to Dar-es-Salaam and which, he says, laid down the return of Nkomo and a few others at some time after the Addis Ababa Conference. Malianga duly left Dar-es-Salaam with Nkomo, although

83

they then made their ways separately. Later Mugabe complained that Nkomo left without telling the executive what to do.

At the end of June Nkomo and Chikerema went to Livingstone to lobby at the Victoria Falls Conference. While in Northern Rhodesia they talked to Kaunda, who, according to Shamuyarira, told them that he disapproved of the exile of the executive in Dar-es-Salaam. While Nkomo was in Northern Rhodesia he met Takawira and Moyo who had come from Dar-es-Salaam. Takawira was supervising some students travelling to Dar-es-Salaam, Moyo was accompanying Mukhahlera, who was ill, back to Southern Rhodesia. It was agreed to hold an executive meeting on 10 July at Shiwa Ngandu in north-east Northern Rhodesia, as had been tentatively planned when Nkomo left Dar-es-Salaam.

During the executive's exile some nationalists in Salisbury had felt frustration through lack of direction and some members of the executive were becoming increasingly dissatisfied with Nkomo's leadership. In the past Nkomo had seemed too vacillating and indecisive. Several felt that the present policy of keeping most of the executive out of the country was wrong. The lack of any organized activity within Southern Rhodesia particularly galled those who felt that the nationalist movement in Southern Rhodesia had achieved very little over the years through indifferent leadership. Nkomo found when he returned from Dar-es-Salaam that meetings of opponents to his leadership had been taking place in the Salisbury townships. After his visit to Northern Rhodesia he found that Marondera, a ZAPU Youth Leader, had carried letters from Mugabe and Takawira in Dar-es-Salaam to those in Salisbury who had held the hostile meetings. Nkomo and Chikerema failed to get a satisfactory explanation from the recipients of the letters, so Nkomo sent a telegram postponing the executive meeting to have been held at Shiwa. Moyo telephoned from Dar-es-Salaam to inform Nkomo that Sithole, Takawira, Malianga and Mugabe had decided to replace Nkomo by Sithole with Takawira as his deputy. Nkomo spoke to a meeting in the Salisbury township of Harare, denouncing eleven men as enemies of the movement and saying that he had heard that the four executive members were in league with them. Then Edson Zvobgo, who had recently returned from representing ZAPU in New York, arrived in Salisbury with letters from Dar-es-Salaam for people in Salisbury. Chikerema heard of this, apprehended and searched him. The letters which he discovered and showed to Nkomo confirmed the apostasy of the four leaders in Dar-es-Salaam. Consequently Nkomo suspended them and sent them a cable containing this information. The next day the seven members of the executive in Dar-es-Salaam met there. The four suspended members deposed Nkomo and elected Sithole in his place. Moyo, C. M. Muchachi and Msika remained loyal to Nkomo and walked out of the meeting. This was the beginning of the split in the nationalist movement which still remains unhealed. The rebellious group, who later formed ZANU, returned from Dar-es-Salaam after three weeks and that was the end for the time being of a ZAPU headquarters abroad. Nkomo's policy of an executive in exile had precipitated a crisis in the party and had provided the unusual conditions in which the party splintered.

Lusaka, 1964 onwards

One of the policies on which the rebels challenged Nkomo was his opposition to forming a new party after ZAPU was banned. Nkomo believed that the Government would strike at a new party as it had at the old and that the nationalist movement would again lose much of its property. The opposition to Nkomo felt that the effective organization of nationalism in Southern Rhodesia was impeded by the lack of a party which would work in the open within the country. The dissidents eventually forced Nkomo's hand when they formed ZANU early in August 1963. His response was to create PCC, nominally not a party, but in fact very much like one. Nkomo and his allies could in PCC organize against ZANU while Nkomo continued to attack the idea of a new nationalist party. Nkomo's supporters abroad still called themselves members of ZAPU. Having what amounted to a party organization in Southern Rhodesia Nkomo and his friends again had to face the problem of what to do if the Government struck at PCC as it had at the three previous parties. The first big onslaught by the Government came in April 1964: instead of banning PCC it restricted Nkomo, the President, with a few of his lieutenants to Gonakudzingwa. This was the first of many restrictions by the Rhodesian Front Government of nationalist leaders to Gonakudzingwa and Wha Wha. The four most experienced members of the PCC hierarchy, on Nkomo's advice, kept out of the country once the Government had shown its intention to shackle the nationalist leaders. At first they fluctuated between Dar-es-Salaam and Lusaka, but by the middle of 1964 they had settled their headquarters in Lusaka. The two most senior men were the pioneers of ANC, Chikerema, who was Deputy President of PCC, and Nyandoro, who was General Secretary. One of their colleagues in Lusaka was J. Z. Moyo, National Treasurer in ZAPU since its inauguration and continuing in this office in PCC. The other member of the quartet was Silundika, PCC's Secretary for Information and Publicity, who had been Secretary General of NDP, although, unlike the other three, not on the ZAPU executive. He had played a rather passive role in the ZAPU era, but had accompanied Nkomo

86

to Livingstone during the Victoria Falls Conference in June 1963.

With these leaders safely away from Southern Rhodesia PCC ensured in the months after Nkomo's restriction that the party had some experienced and senior leaders to conduct a nationalist fight, even if cut off from domestic politics. The Government had removed all the remaining members of the PCC executive from circulation, as well as many lesser figures, by the time it banned both PCC and ZANU in August 1964. After that political activity became almost impossible in Southern Rhodesia for the nationalists. PCC at least had during this period of increasing paralysis within the country a strong headquarters just outside it in Lusaka. The intention was not to direct the internal nationalist movement from abroad. This was scarcely practicable, and in any case Nkomo was still controlling PCC, in theory and to some extent in practice, from restriction in Gonakudzingwa. Until the State of Emergency declared for the Gonakudzingwa area just before UDI in November 1965 Nkomo received many visitors, most of whom were political sympathizers. The function of the Lusaka headquarters was to coordinate overseas activities. Also the four leaders themselves kept up pressure on the British Government and on those who might help their cause. They were available too for a constitutional conference if Britain should call one, an unlikely but possible contingency. The exiled leaders were able from Lusaka to maintain an authoritative stream of PCC/ZAPU propaganda by press statements and press conferences. They frequently broadcast in the vernacular languages from Lusaka to Africans in Southern Rhodesia, urging them to implement nationalist policies. In Lusaka the headquarters staff were sufficiently close to Southern Rhodesia to obtain information and to meet Africans leaving or going to Southern Rhodesia. Some of these leaders played a role in organizing the movements of guerillas between foreign military training camps and Southern Rhodesia.

A UDI became more likely after Smith became Prime Minister in April 1964 and the Lusaka exiles, like their Dar-es-Salaam predecessors, talked of countering such a declaration of independence by setting up a government-in-exile. Moyo in September 1964 said that the four in Lusaka would form the nucleus of such a government. One wonders where the other particles were to come from. Chikerema in October 1965 claimed that plans were ready for setting up a government-in-exile immediately in the event of UDI. Envoys would go to sixty countries to request recognition. As the ban on the nationalist parties persisted into 1965 and as the whole movement at home and abroad was in a state of atrophy, a UDI seemed one hope of resuscitating ZANU and PCC/ZAPU. Such a challenge by the Rhodesian Government might mobilize world support for the nationalists and incite their supporters at home. The headquarters of ZAPU in Lusaka could convert itself into a government-in-exile which many states would recognize as the legitimate government. The actuality of UDI was different. The world was indignant, but most forgot the nationalists, whose failure so far had lost them the respect of those who might have helped them. Most Africans in Rhodesia took UDI quietly. The Government and police had iron control. There was no sustained, widespread, organized rising. And the ZAPU exiles in Lusaka, in spite of having looked forward for so long to becoming a government-in-exile if the Rhodesian Government seized independence, seemingly had no prepared plan to declare themselves a government and to seek recognition. On the day of UDI Moyo, who was in London, made a statement which repeated the familiar charges against Britain and made the usual predictions of bloodshed and catastrophe in Rhodesia. He did not say that the ZAPU leaders had instantaneously formed themselves into a government-in-exile as soon as the Rhodesian Government illegally declared independence. He explained that he and his colleagues would hold a meeting in Lusaka the following day and their decision whether to form a government-in-exile would depend on certain external factors, including the reaction of the British Government. In fact nothing more was heard of ZAPU's intention to form a government-in-exile.

ZANU's centres overseas, 1964 onwards

When Nkomo was restricted in April 1964, Sithole, the leader of ZANU, remained free. When the Government began soon after to move against ZANU it was still less severe than on PCC. But when the two parties were banned each was put on an equal footing of impotence. All the ZANU leaders in Southern Rhodesia were held by the Government. Several were abroad, but ZANU established nothing comparable to the PCC/ZAPU headquarters in Lusaka. Dar-es-Salaam became a centre for ZANU leaders, and from there Mukono organized military training abroad for guerilla recruits. When Smith declared independence ZANU demonstrated their pathetic frailty by announcing that they had immediately formed a government at Sikombela, where the Rhodesian Government held many of the ZANU leaders in restriction. 'From now on where the leader of the people, the magnanimous Reverend Sithole is, there the seat of the Government of the people will be.' Chitepo, the National Chairman, had for several years been Director of Public Prosecutions in Tanzania. He did not play an active and regular part in Rhodesian nationalist politics during this period, but after UDI he gave up his Tanzanian job and moved to Lusaka to take charge of ZANU's external activities. There he briefed ZANU guerillas before they left for Rhodesia. Also, like the PCC/ZAPU leaders, he travelled abroad for his party from the base at Lusaka.

Conclusion

The gap between the ambitions and the achievements of the two parties' high commands abroad remained large. It may be symbolized by contrasting the success of the Rhodesian Government in maintaining an independent rebel regime with a vain injunction broadcast by Chikerema from Zambia to Rhodesian Africans after UDI: 'Take your bows, your axe, your spear, and smash that Government.'

6
Ambassadors

Overseas offices: functions and publications

Not only did the Southern Rhodesian nationalists send some
of their leaders abroad in times of crisis, but they also posted
ambassadors to foreign capitals on a permanent footing.
Mainly in independent African states the Southern Rhodesian nationalist parties established offices which were run
by accredited representatives.

We have seen how in London the permanent mission
worked in cooperation with temporary emissaries. In 1960
and 1961, the headquarters overseas and the London office
were indistinguishable. First Nkomo, then Takawira, headed
NDP's organization overseas from the London office. When
Takarwira left, the London office continued its functions as
an office, although ceasing to be the headquarters of the
movement abroad.

The London office was the first one to be established overseas. Its purpose was clear, to provide a continuous organization for exerting pressure directly or indirectly on the
British Government. The functions of the other, later offices
are less obvious, but they seemed to have aimed principally
at arousing public opinion abroad to sympathy with the
Southern Rhodesian nationalists, and at stirring governments to support their cause in various international

forums, like the United Nations and the various Pan-African organizations. To stimulate interest in Southern Rhodesia the representatives around the world issued press statements which were used by newspapers in the countries of their origin and sometimes by those further afield. The Communist Chinese Agency, Hsinhua, frequently picked up Southern Rhodesian nationalist propaganda from the office in Cairo. The representatives in foreign capitals were able to explain the significance of the latest iniquities of the Southern Rhodesian Government, and consequently at each crisis to stoke up popular and governmental indignation in the host country. It does not seem that those who were purely representatives were much concerned to wring money from local sources, including governments. This task was usually entrusted to the more senior members of the movement.

Several of the foreign offices produced duplicated periodicals for circulation to sympathizers within the country of origin. These publications also helped to maintain the enthusiasm for the nationalist cause of Southern Rhodesian Africans living in foreign countries, but not actively engaged in extra-territorial politics; for example, the London periodicals reached Southern Rhodesian Africans studying in England, and the Lusaka periodicals were read by emigrants from Southern Rhodesia who worked in Northern Rhodesia. Some of the overseas branches sent copies of their regular propaganda back to the homeland itself. The Southern Rhodesian Government thought it worth while banning in September 1962 *Zimbabwe News*, published in Cairo in newspaper format at irregular intervals of at least a month from May 1962, and Vol. 1, No. 6, of *Spear*, which emanated from London.

After *Zimbabwe News* the Cairo office produced a printed periodical (most of the Southern Rhodesian nationalist journals inside and outside the country were duplicated) called *Zimbabgwe Review*. After the split this supported Nkomo. ZANU in Cairo had their own *Zimbabwe Today*. The other foreign outposts, besides London and Cairo, which produced periodicals were Dar-es-Salaam and Lusaka. All, somewhat confusingly, called one of their periodicals *Zimbabwe Review* (although Cairo spelled it with a 'g') and two, the London and Dar-es-Salaam *Zimbabwe Reviews*, used the same block for the front page title. The Lusaka version appeared weekly, at least through much of 1965. By February 1966 the Dar-es-Salaam version had run to more than eight volumes of ten numbers each. All these originated from ZAPU offices, but in Dar-es-Salaam, Lusaka and London ZANU have had their own organs. At the time of the split in Dar-es-Salaam two different publications appeared there, both called *Zimbabwe Today* : one supported Nkomo, the other opposed him. All these periodicals exhibit the industry of the nationalists resident in foreign capitals, but the nationalists probably reached larger audiences more effectively by broadcasts. As we have seen, the London representatives, as well as visiting leaders, appeared on television. From Cairo the Southern Rhodesian nationalists were able to broadcast in the vernacular languages to Africans in Southern Rhodesia. ZANU broadcast on Radio Zambia and urged Africans at home to support the guerillas' fight for freedom.

A case study: the Dar-es-Salaam Zimbabwe Review

A short analysis of one source of overseas propaganda, the Dar-es-Salaam *Zimbabwe Review* from 1964 to 1966, will give some idea of the tone and content of the Southern Rhodesian nationalists' publications abroad, while drawing attention to some interesting features peculiar to this periodical. Between April 1964 and February 1966 over fifty numbers appeared, and between July 1964 and March 1965 these were at roughly weekly intervals. Most of the articles were in English, but, like the Lusaka *Zimbabwe Review*, there were some in Shona and Ndebele, the vernacular languages of Southern Rhodesia.

In its range of tone and material the Dar-es-Salaam *Zimbabwe Review* was narrower than several of the other overseas periodicals, as it had a higher proportion of virulent effervescence to factual reporting. The themes of its articles were typical of the Southern Rhodesian nationalists in exile. Like all of the nationalists' publications abroad, it gave news of events in Southern Rhodesia, of the British Government's policies on Southern Rhodesia and of the nationalists' activities abroad.

Much of the internal news concerned politically inspired violence by Africans against persons and property. All the overseas periodicals praised this violence as a patriotic activity, and made the most of each small event. (A headline in the London *Zimbabwe Review* of August-September 1966 read '75 Goats Killed'.) The nationalists writing in Dar-es-Salaam, like their comrades elsewhere, seemed unsure whether the Africans in Southern Rhodesia were on the brink of a bloody revolution caused by the intransigence of the British and Southern Rhodesian Governments, or whether the revolution had arrived. However, stirring exhortations to intensify the fight flowed regularly from Dar-es-Salaam and the other offices. 'Comrades and fellow fighters, sharpen your arrows, pull tight your bow cords, axes must be poised for the last kill, for, the liberation lies in our hands and our sweat and blood.' 'Combat the most hideous and heinous foe you have ever faced and let him quack [sic] in his boots—for the vengeance of Zimbabweans is just and righteous.' An editorial in

94

December 1964 asserted that the revolution had entered a new and bitter stage and that more were going to die (although not, presumably, in Dar-es-Salaam). 'The only way to freedom is through bullets.' (The Lusaka *Zimbabwe Review* in May 1965 predicted race war in the event of a UDI, in which some Africans would die.)

A stream of unrestrained abuse was directed against the Rhodesian Front, a 'murderous gang of blood-thirsty farmers', 'of untamed political lunatics', led by 'a diabolic maniac hedged in by his own priggishness'. The police were characterized as brutal racialists. Repeatedly the Government was dubbed Nazi or Fascist (a common accusation by the exiled nationalists) and wildly accused of appropriate crimes and intentions. Here Dar-es-Salaam showed a more inflamed imagination than the other foreign outposts. The Rhodesian Government's behaviour to the Africans was implicitly compared with the Nazis' persecution of the Jews. Warders killed the babies of women in restricted areas. Soldiers killed, raped and pillaged rural Africans. Smith was using the Nazi methods of mass torture and mass murder to exterminate the race. Hundreds of Africans were frozen to death. Others suffocated in new gas chambers in Salisbury.

The masochistic nationalist fantasy was accompanied by a Marxist interpretation of Southern Rhodesian politics. Particularly from about November 1964 ZAPU propaganda from Dar-es-Salaam was more self-consciously and precisely Marxist than any other Southern Rhodesian nationalist literature. In January 1965 *Zimbabwe Review* claimed that it had 'broadened its scope and [stood] up as a Vanguard Magazine'. The 'peasant masses' and workers of Zimbabwe were seen to be in a revolutionary struggle against imperialism, colonialism and neo-colonialism. Victory for this revolution was inevitable, as the 'Great October Revolution' and revolutionary successes in Cuba and Zanzibar demonstrated. The Zimbabwe revolution aiming at a class-less society was an integral part of a world struggle. The Chiefs, always denounced by the other overseas periodicals, were 'puppet reactionaries'. One edition of the Dar-es-Salaam *Zimbabwe Review* finished with an exhortation which neatly fused tribal and Christian with Marxist influences: 'Sons and daughters of Zimbabwe, we have nothing to lose but the chains. Let us not betray the revolution. Preach the gospel of revolution to all and sundry.'

The militancy of this Dar-es-Salaam propaganda, while uniquely extreme, reflected the frustration expressed by all the nationalists abroad, particularly since 1964. Typical also of Southern Rhodesian nationalism in this period were the fierce denunciations of the British Government for trying to help Smith by seeking compromises, of West Germany for aiding the Rhodesian Government, and of ZANU as a tool of imperialism.

Where, why and when overseas offices existed

The most flourishing overseas offices were in London and the three African capitals of Cairo, Lusaka and Dar-es-Salaam. But the nationalists at various times had agents also in New York, Accra, Algiers and Blantyre. Largely as a result of Nkomo's preparatory work the first overseas post after London was established at Cairo early in November 1960. Silundika, who had left Southern Rhodesia in July 1960 after the riots, in spite of police attempts to prevent him, was appointed Director of the Cairo office. In October 1960 he had been elected to the NDP executive as Secretary General. Silundika did not spend long in Cairo, for he took part in the Federal Review Conference in London in December 1960 and was active in Southern Rhodesia from the middle of January 1961. He was officially replaced in

Cairo by Washington Malianga in May 1961. Malianga remained there until, with the formation of ZAPU in December 1961, he, like Takawira in London, was recalled to Southern Rhodesia, where he succeeded Silundika, his predecessor in Cairo, as party Secretary General. ZAPU has had several more representatives in Cairo. Edward Ndlovu moved there from the Accra office in 1962. Tasiana Mutizwa, who edited *Zimbabwe News* in 1962, was acting representative in early 1963. The next full representative was Tranos Makombe, who left a lucrative job with a mining company to serve ZAPU in Cairo. When the party split, Makombe joined ZANU, but stayed in Cairo until recalled by ZANU to be on the national executive as Secretary for Pan-African and External Affairs. ZANU reopened their office in Cairo in January 1964 when they sent out Moton Malianga, an experienced political traveller abroad who had been Deputy President of NDP. PCC/ZAPU had a rival office with first R. Sibanda from 1963 to 1964, then Stephen Nkomo, brother of the leader, and finally D. S. Mpongo, who had worked in the Cairo office for a few years, in charge. It is perhaps significant that the Southern Rhodesian nationalists sent several senior party men to Egypt as ambassadors. Silundika, the two Maliangas and Makombe all attained executive rank during their political careers. The choice of Nkomo's brother as a representative in Cairo may also indicate that the nationalists wished specially to cultivate the U.A.R. Government. Possibly Nasser was prepared to help and finance the Southern Rhodesian nationalists if they sent authoritative supplicants. Cairo was an obvious place for African nationalists to seek sympathy. The U.A.R. was an early leader of the anti-colonialist, ex-colony, neutralist third world. Several international conferences were held there. Geographically it lay at the intersection of African, Arab and Asian nationalisms.

97

G

For the Southern Rhodesian nationalists Cairo was an airport through which many would pass in flying from Salisbury to London, New York and Asia. This may have helped to foster and sustain interest in Cairo as a base for overseas activities.

Dar-es-Salaam, even more than Cairo, was a natural home for African nationalists. Nyerere encouraged exiles from other African countries to establish bases in his capital. PAFMECSA operated from there. For the Southern Rhodesian nationalists Dar-es-Salaam was relatively close to home and, when NDP first sent a representative, J. M. Chirimbani, to Dar-es-Salaam towards the end of 1961, Tanganyika was the nearest self-governing English-speaking African nationalist state. From September 1962 till July 1963 ZAPU established its headquarters overseas in Dar-es-Salaam where it already had established an office. The ZAPU representative from at least 1963 (possibly from 1962 when Chirimbani left) was B. S. Madlela. At his death in February 1965 he was succeeded by F. Nehwati. In the first part of 1964 Nyandoro and Chikerema spent some time in Dar-es-Salaam, giving the office there a temporary special importance. For a longer time some of the ZANU leaders, like H. Hamadziripi, Under Secretary for External Affairs, gravitated to Dar-es-Salaam, where the party also had a representative, E. M. Pasipanodya. In the second half of 1966 L. P. Chihota took over from him.

In Lusaka as in Dar-es-Salaam ZAPU had an office before they set up a headquarters. Lusaka was even more conveniently geographically than Dar-es-Salaam and the association between the nationalist movements north and south of the Zambesi was close. Yet it was only in May 1962 that Nkomo announced that ZAPU was about to have an office in Lusaka. PCC/ZAPU had a representative (A. Ngwenya in 1964, Dube in 1965) in Lusaka even when

Silundika (till mid-1964) and the four members of the executive (from mid-1964) were resident there. ZANU were also represented in Northern Rhodesia, from February 1964 by S. Parirewa, who was expelled by the Government later in the year. Significantly, PCC/ZAPU never had an accredited representative in Nyasaland, where Banda favoured ZANU, but ZANU's chief official was first J. A. Mawere, then Percy Ntini.

The other three overseas offices, even more geographically remote from Southern Rhodesia than Cairo, were in Accra, Algiers and New York. Ghana was an obvious place to seek support as Nkrumah had worked hard for the leadership of radical Pan-Africanism. Independent in 1957, prominent in the United Nations, in the Accra Conferences of 1958 and in the Casablanca bloc, Ghana set the pace for many African nationalist movements. Nkomo made contact in Ghana before NDP set up an office. By the end of 1961 Edward Ndlovu was representing NDP in Accra. After he left in the following year there seems to have been a gap in Southern Rhodesian representation there until mid-1964 when Sibanda came from Cairo to open an office for PCC/ZAPU. By November 1964, when the ZAPU representative made a press statement claiming that the Chiefs did not speak for other Africans in supporting the Government's bid for immediate independence, ZANU had Davies M'gabe in Accra to make a separate but similar statement.

Like Ghana, Algeria made a vivid impression on struggling, militant African nationalists. Southern Rhodesian Africans compared the fierce and bloody Algerian war between white settlers and indigenous people with what could happen in Southern Rhodesia if concessions were not made to African demands. Both countries had strong, entrenched white minorities with vested economic interests. These facts partly explain ZAPU's appointment of M. M. Noko

99

as representative in Algiers in mid-1964. Also by this date Algeria, like Ghana, had probably helped to train Southern Rhodesian Africans as guerilla fighters.

Only two overseas representatives of the Southern Rhodesian African nationalists resided outside Africa. One was in London, a special case, the other in New York. None of the work at the United Nations seems to have been done by New York representatives and it seems possible that ZAPU had an official in New York partly because Edson Zvobgo, the first appointee there, was studying in the United States. In New York as in Ghana, however, Nkomo had been a visitor and may have laid the foundations in 1960 for an office there. In June 1963 Zvobgo returned from America to Africa, where in Dar-es-Salaam and Salisbury he helped the conspiracy against Nkomo. After his defection PCC/ZAPU sent Sibanda to New York in 1964 and L. K. Dube in 1965.

It is difficult to see what the representatives in New York did for the nationalists, as they do not seem to have approached the American Government in Washington. One function may have been to act as a focus of loyalty for other African students from Southern Rhodesia. Wherever there was any concentration of Southern Rhodesian Africans living away from home the representative helped to organize them and stimulate their nationalist fervour— Mutasa for ZANU and Nelson Samkange for ZAPU wrote circular letters to their countrymen in London urging them to meet and to work for the cause in England. The Lusaka quartet tried to provide leadership to the large Southern Rhodesian African community in Northern Rhodesia. Here, as in London, properly organized branches of the nationalist parties existed, each with its own officials. Usually the branches would look to the representative for guidance, although in May 1964 the ZANU representative suspended the Chairman of the Blantyre branch.

Whatever the objective value of the overseas offices may have been to the Southern Rhodesian nationalist movement, their existence was of psychological value when the nationalist parties at home were labouring under unusually severe difficulties. It is informative to compare the similar reactions of Nkomo and Dumbutshena after ZAPU was banned in 1962 and of Shamuyarira after ZANU was banned in 1964. All stated, in the face of crushing defeat at home, that the activities of the overseas branches would be increased. The web of foreign offices at least gave the nationalists the feeling that all their organization had not been paralysed by the Government.

Political visits

In contrast to the continuous work of the established offices were odd visits of individual nationalists. Although much of the Southern Rhodesian Africans' overseas travelling was undertaken for specific purposes like attending conferences, they occasionally visited other countries for less definite aims like fostering friendly relations and learning from others' political experience. The political dividends of such visits were often speculative, although, like the propaganda of the offices abroad, they might help to win friends who would attack the Southern Rhodesian Government in international forums. Some of the most constructive of these somewhat undirected expeditions were Nkomo's to African countries in 1959 and 1960 when he was arousing fellow Africans' sensitivity to the nationalists' predicament in Southern Rhodesia. Sometimes the leaders planned journeys of political sight-seeing, like Takawira's tour of West Africa in 1961. Sometimes, on the way to perform a specific task abroad, they broke their journey at a point en route to make or strengthen a political bond; for example, Sithole, returning to his base at Dar-es-Salaam from the United Nations late in 1962, stopped in Cairo and made a press statement.

The nationalists and Communist countries

The nationalists' visits to Communist countries, like those to independent African states, were probably motivated by curiosity about the political systems of fellow anti-colonialists and by the hope of converting their natural sympathy into positive support. Often quite junior officials went to the Communist world, like T. S. Moyo, the Deputy Treasurer of ZAPU, who visited Jugoslavia, and Alfred Gondo, who, although not on the national executive, represented ZAPU in China in March and April 1963. It seems that Egypt was one place where the Communists met Southern Rhodesian Africans to invite them to their countries. Three Cairo representatives went on trips to Communist states. Moton Malianga went to China; so did Makombe as the guest of the Committee of the Afro-Asian Peoples' Solidarity Organization in August 1963; and E. S. Elunduku was in Moscow in July 1962 and North Korea the following September. In addition, M. B. Gumbo, who was attached to the Cairo office from July 1960 to June 1961, visited China. Chikerema, when Deputy President of PCC/ZAPU, visited China in January 1964 at the invitation of the Chinese People's Institute of Foreign Affairs. According to Dupont, the Southern Rhodesian Minister of Justice. PCC/ZAPU were in contact with the Chinese in Dar-es-Salaam at this period and received £7000 from them. In 1964 Nyandoro and Moyo went to North Korea during a trip which included the United States, West Germany and India.

The Southern Rhodesian Government has always accused the African nationalists of Communist sympathies, particularly since Smith has been Prime Minister. The visits in themselves prove nothing. The Communist powers, of course, support the nationalists, for they are regarded as combatants in the struggle against imperialism. Equally natural is the nationalists' friendliness to Communist Governments who support their cause. Certainly the Southern Rhodesian nationalists were not Communists either before or after the visits of a few of their members to Communist countries, except according to the definition accepted by many Southern African Europeans who equate Communism with almost any fundamental opposition to their own ideas of 'white civilization'. Like all African nationalists the Southern Rhodesians sometimes use Marxist or quasi-Marxist jargon in attacking European regimes in Africa without becoming Marxists. The strength of Marxist influence on the Dar-es-Salaam *Zimbabwe Review* is exceptional in Southern Rhodesian nationalist propaganda, at home or abroad. No doubt the Southern Rhodesian nationalists welcome Communist support at the United Nations or in any other way, and they may have received money from the Chinese. More important is the extent to which Communist states provided training and weapons for potential guerilla fighters. This active help needs to be discussed alongside similar services provided by some African states. To the extent that the Southern Rhodesian nationalists abroad have organized the training and directed the fighting of what they call 'freedom fighters' and the Southern Rhodesian Government calls 'terrorists', their activities have passed beyond the pseudo-diplomatic to the pseudo-revolutionary.

7
Planning violence

Arms and military training from abroad

After the nationalist movement had been repeatedly frustrated in attempts to win its objectives by peaceful means some nationalists in Southern Rhodesia decided that the white minority would yield only if pure politics were backed by force. Political violence on any scale required foreign assistance, for the Africans lacked military material and training. Several states were prepared to train Africans from Southern Rhodesia in guerilla fighting and sabotage and to send into the country supplies of arms and ammunition. Throughout the history of nationalism in Southern Rhodesia, violence against people and property smouldered and occasionally burst into flame. But only in mid-1962 did some nationalist leaders decide to accept military help from abroad (Shamuyarira, 1965, 201-202). The Zimbabwe Liberation Army, a militant organization promising violence, started publicizing itself in September 1962 just before ZAPU was banned. It distributed leaflets in Salisbury and Bulawayo signed by 'General Chedu', who was in fact two members of the ZAPU executive and a Youth Leader, although the ZAPU leadership always publicly dissociated itself from the Zimbabwe Liberation Army's acts of violence. This 'Army' does not seem to have used foreign weapons in 1962, although it was rumoured that ten Southern Rhodesian Africans who served in the Zimbabwe Liberation Army had trained with the F.L.N. in Algeria. It is possible that some Africans left the country in 1962 for military training in Algeria, Ghana, Czechoslovakia and China.

From December 1962 information about the military aid which the nationalists received from abroad is less conjectural. The police and security forces found men who had clandestinely entered and arms which had been secretly brought into Southern Rhodesia. Arrested Africans made statements to their captors and in court.

Russian and Chinese arms and explosives were smuggled into Southern Rhodesia from Northern Rhodesia and hidden in dumps around the country. Some cases will illustrate these activities. In May 1963 the police found three cases of plastic explosive, a hundred detonators and three time fuses in a car that had come from Northern Rhodesia. Three PCC/ZAPU members were arrested in Northern Rhodesia en route for the south with explosives bearing Russian marks of origin. An arms cache in the Bulawayo area, found early in 1964, contained time pencils, hand grenades, automatic weapons and detonators, with an instruction book marked in Chinese. This collection was brought by two men from Northern Rhodesia. In August 1964 a group of PCC men from Salisbury were jailed for possessing Russian grenades. In February 1965 both ZAPU and ZANU asked OAU for arms and the Liberation Committee promised to grant these requests.

Besides supplying war materials to the nationalists some states hostile to the Southern Rhodesian Government invited Africans to learn how to use them. The recruits for the nationalists' irregular armies left and returned to Southern Rhodesia via Northern Rhodesia. Chikerema stated in Lusaka on 20 February 1964: 'If Field does anything funny [declares unilateral independence] we'll have soldiers marching across those borders. And I don't mean foreign soldiers. We have no need for foreign help—we have our own soldiers.' On 6 May 1964 the Ministry of Law and Order published a statement which revealed some of the facts behind Chikerema's hyperbole. The source of the Government's information was Africans who had gone to North Africa for training but had become disillusioned. The trainees left Southern Rhodesia and travelled ostensibly as refugees or scholarship holders through Northern Rhodesia, Dar-es-Salaam, Nairobi and Cairo to the training camps. The Government estimated that over fifty per cent deserted after the training. The deserters explained that before training they had been promised high ranks in 'freedom armies' and were consequently disappointed that they were expected after training to operate alone without pay or equipment. They complained at the incompetence of the nationalist leaders they met abroad (whether Southern Rhodesian or not is not specified). One said, 'they could not organize a football match, let alone a revolution'.

Many of the Southern Rhodesian Africans who received military training overseas were not disillusioned, as the Government has implicitly acknowledged in its statements about the danger of terrorists infiltrating into Southern Rhodesia across the Zambesi. Some of those who went to foreign training camps returned to Northern Rhodesia and waited. Others continued to Southern Rhodesia and risked arrest for their exploits or for possessing arms illegally.

From September 1964 to March 1965 about forty Africans from ZANU received military training in Ghana. ZANU officials in Malawi and Dar-es-Salaam provided travel documents for the recruits. Until November 1964 Ghanaian instructors trained them in a camp at Half Assini, and then they moved to Obenamasi, where they trained with other Africans under Ghanaian and Chinese instructors. They learned sabotage, guerilla warfare and the manufacture of explosives. Mukono, a senior ZANU official based on Dar-es-Salaam, supervised the whole scheme, while Parirewa, who had earlier been expelled from Zambia, managed its operation in Ghana. In March 1965 the trained men received detailed instructions from Mukono at Mbeya, on the border of Tanzania and Zambia. The men were divided into nine groups of about five, each group having a leader, a code name (e.g. Hippo) and an area of Rhodesia to work in. Their orders were to attack European farms, to kill Europeans, to organize the people in the struggle for independence, and to disrupt the May 1965 General Election by sabotage and attacks on Europeans. Arrangements were made for each group to keep in contact with officials outside Rhodesia. From April 1965 the guerillas crossed into Rhodesia, where thirty-four were eventually arrested. In court the accused unconvincingly claimed that they had been tricked into going for military training by the offer of scholarships and had no intention of carrying out the instructions.

ZAPU were as zealous as ZANU in obtaining professional advice about undermining the government. Between March 1964 and October 1965 each of fifty-two Rhodesian Africans took part in one of six training programmes, four in Moscow, one in Nanking and one in Pyongyang, North Korea. The subjects of instruction included: the intelligence services of Britain, U.S.A., France and West Germany; the techniques of intelligence agents, such as radio communication, photographing documents and recruiting helpers; the use of arms and explosives; and political science. Several members of ZAPU in Lusaka, including at least two of the headquarters staff, Moyo and Chikerema, organized the movements .of the Africans to the training centres and to Rhodesia itself. They were recruited in Zambia and returned there after training. ZAPU officials briefed them, drove them to the Zambian-Rhodesian frontier which they were to cross, and tried to organize communications between them once they were in Rhodesia. Twenty-four were later arrested and appeared in court. Two pleaded that they had been misled by offers of free education, and one claimed that he had trained for a role in a future African government.

Action by guerillas

On 29 April 1966 the first clash occurred between guerillas and soldiers in what one ZANU spokesman described as 'the great battle at Sinoia'. A band of about twenty trained ZANU fighters, after crossing the Zambesi in mid-April, moved south in the direction of Sinoia and Salisbury. One of its objects seems to have been to cut off the electricity supply running from the Kariba Dam to Salisbury. In pursuit of this aim they attempted to blow up a pylon by attaching a bomb to it. Their main purpose failed, although they damaged the pylon. According to ZANU, the group attacked a temporary police station twenty-five miles north of Sinoia, which was guarding the power line, and killed five policemen. The police denied that they had lost any men. The attack on the pylon led security forces to search for the saboteurs in that area. They eventually found them and engaged with the help of a helicopter in a running battle with them. Seven nationalists were killed. ZANU claimed to have killed twenty-five members of the security forces and to have shot down two helicopters, but this report was not substantiated from any other sources and seems doubtful. According to the official statement, the guerillas, trained in China and under instructions from Chitepo, fought with Russian and Chinese weapons, and carried Chinese publications.

On 1 April another ZANU group infiltrated into Rhodesia. It split into three and the largest subdivision, of six men, travelled towards the Midlands, possibly hoping to make contact with Sithole, the President of ZANU, who was restricted to Sikombela, near Gwelo, in an area large enough to make a clandestine meeting possible. This group was responsible for killing a European farmer and his wife, the Viljoens, on an isolated farm near Hartley. The police found ZANU pamphlets at the scene of the murders. The Government claimed to have killed or captured all six of this band in the following months. The Viljoen murders resembled the killing of another European, P. J. A. Oberholzer, in the Melsetter area in July 1964, by the ZANU 'Crocodile Gang', who had also come in from Zambia.

One of the two other subsections of the ZANU group which arrived in Rhodesia at the beginning of April 1966 consisted of two members, who went towards the Fort Victoria area. The other subsection of five headed for the Eastern district with orders to blow up the oil pipeline between Beira, Mozambique, and Umtali. All seven were captured and tried. They had been trained in guerilla warfare in Peking, Egypt and Tanzania, and possessed Russian and Chinese arms, including sub-machine guns, grenades and T.N.T. They also carried ZANU pamphlets, which called for the blood of European farmers and the destruction of their property, and which were to be left at the scenes of action. ZANU leaders in Zambia instructed the guerillas to attack white farmers (one guerilla quoted Mukono's command not to kill Europeans in the streets, but farmers because they supported the Government), to fight white police and soldiers, and to disrupt the working of government. In court those accused claimed that they had acted in order to overturn the post-UDI 'rebel regime' and restore constitutional rule by force. They consequently demanded to be treated as prisoners-of-war and refused to recognize the jurisdiction of the court, because it acted under the aegis of a government without legality.

In the last third of 1966 news of further meetings between guerillas and security forces, often in the Zambesi valley, came from both nationalist and Government sources, both sides claiming victories at each announcement. Further trials revealed that ninety Africans had been to Algeria for military training in 1965 and that Tanzania had provided training in weapons and explosives.

Conclusion

The potentiality of the nationalists' irregular soldiers has so far exceeded their achievements by a substantial margin. In May 1966 the Rhodesian Government estimated that between five and six hundred terrorists were waiting in Zambia and three hundred in Tanzania. This estimate, like similar ones made by the Government from November 1965 onwards, may have been exaggerated through fear of the unknown or by the desire to justify the Government's intention to declare a state of emergency. If the figures were true the nationalists scarcely had an army. If the figures were somewhat inflated they still had the skilled military manpower to cause an unpleasant disruption of Rhodesian white society. As yet the impact of the guerilla bands has been small. Handfuls of irregular soldiers have met strong and vigilant security forces, especially in the Zambesi valley. The Rhodesian Government claimed that it arrested eighty trained terrorists in the year before UDI and that it killed or captured about a hundred between April and

December 1966. It believes that it has dealt with nearly all who have entered the country. The nationalists claim greater success, but, compared with the rebel army in Algeria or Mau Mau in Kenya, they have accomplished little. They have not remotely approached their objective of overthrowing the Government.

8

Nkomo the traveller

The first chapter briefly and in general terms placed the various kinds of international activity of the Southern Rhodesian nationalists in the context of the historical development of the nationalist movement. Subsequent chapters have examined in more detail each section of overseas action in turn. This chapter will re-integrate the various sections into an interlocking whole by relating chronologically the story of one man's movements, those of Nkomo. Although his activities abroad were until mid-1963 exceptionally numerous and diverse, his political life overseas epitomizes that of the movement he led. This account of Nkomo's travels will show how he (and some of his colleagues) moved frequently from one country to another, varying the tactics of international lobbying.

A narration of Nkomo's journeys is bound to raise the questions, asked (and answered) by his opponents in the Southern Rhodesian nationalist movement, whether all his journeys were really necessary and whether his frequent departures to foreign capitals constituted the most effective form of leadership of the party at home. Did Nkomo spend so much time out of his homeland partly because he feared Government persecution and because he liked travel? If ZANU were right that Nkomo should for the sake of the nationalist movement have stayed in Southern Rhodesia more, does this criticism rub off on many of Nkomo's friends and rivals who were often scarcely less internationally minded than he? This chapter will serve both to draw together the threads of the analysis so far and to point forward to an evaluation in the final chapter of the Southern Rhodesian nationalists' international relations.

Nkomo's international career, 1958-1963

Nkomo's first sortie abroad in the modern era of Southern Rhodesian nationalism was to Ghana whence he returned to Salisbury in August 1958. The main purpose of this visit was to examine a Ghanaian educational trust which awarded bursaries for Africans to study overseas. Nkomo was interested in copying this scheme in his own country.

His next journey overseas, again to Ghana, was politically much more important. In December 1958 Nkomo attended the first Conference of the All African Peoples' Organization in Accra. After this meeting he did not immediately return home and, when his party, ANC, was banned and the other leaders imprisoned on 26 February 1959, he was in Cairo for an Afro-Asian Peoples' Solidarity Council meeting. It is said that the detained ANC leaders in Southern Rhodesia smuggled a message to Nkomo, urging him to stay abroad and carry on the fight there rather than return to restriction where he, like them, would be politically impotent. Acting on this advice or on his own initiative, Nkomo stayed out of Southern Rhodesia and decided to make London his headquarters. He arrived there on 19 March 1959 and lived there intermittently until his return to Salisbury in November 1960. On first arriving in England he addressed public meetings at the Royal Albert Hall and Central Hall, London, and in Birmingham. In August 1959

Nkomo returned to Africa, as an observer at the meeting in Monrovia of the Foreign Ministers of independent African states. From there he moved on to Guinea where he spent several days in Conakry. After this he paid another visit to Accra, travelled to Addis Ababa, and was back in Cairo in September. Before the end of the year Nkomo made a two month lecture tour of the United States, sometimes addressing eight meetings a day. In January 1960 he announced the formation in London of the Southern Rhodesian African Congress Committee Abroad, and in the same month attended the All African Peoples' Conference in Tunis. A new party, NDP, had just started at home and many of those arrested in the Emergency of February 1959 had been released. But Nyandoro and Chikerema, leaders of similar status to Nkomo, remained in captivity. Nkomo stayed out of the reach of Whitehead's police. In April 1960 he visited several independent African countries and in July was a guest when Ghana celebrated becoming a Republic. Although back in London soon after this he returned to Accra the following month to address the World Assembly of Youth. In October 1960 he made his first appearance at the United Nations headquarters in New York, although merely as an unofficial observer. At the end of October the first NDP Congress elected Nkomo President and urgently requested him to return home. He replied that he would come as soon as practicable. This eventually proved to be 20 November, although he left London on 8 November. On the way he attended the installation of Azikwe as Governor-General of Nigeria and saw Mboya as he passed through Kenya. The Government had decided not to seize Nkomo on his arrival, and he, unlike Nyandoro and Chikerema, was free to move round the country.

In just over a week, on 28 November 1960, Nkomo returned to London hoping to secure invitations to conferences on Federation and on Southern Rhodesia. He achieved this aim and took the opportunity of the presence of Banda and Kaunda in London to confer with them. Nkomo attended the Federal Review Conference until he walked out, but Whitehead excluded him from the Conference on Southern Rhodesia which immediately followed. This exclusion led to the rapid abandoning of the Conference in London, but a new one which Nkomo could attend was arranged in Salisbury. Nkomo returned to Southern Rhodesia just before Christmas 1960.

Before the constitutional Conference which started at the end of January 1961 Nkomo twice left the country. First he went to Nairobi for a summit conference of PAFMECA and later to Tanganyika for a meeting of the Steering Committee of the All African Peoples' Organization, of which he was a member. The constitutional Conference took place in Salisbury between 30 January and 7 February. A week later Nkomo flew to London to discipline Takawira, the NDP overseas chief, who had publicly denounced the constitutional agreement to which Nkomo was party. While in London Nkomo also saw Sandys, who had chaired the constitutional Conference, to try to persuade him to change the proposed constitution which Nkomo, like Takawira, now thought inadequate. At the end of February Nkomo left London and on 1 March met Nasser and Kaunda in Damascus. On 7 March Nkomo arrived back in Salisbury after stopping in Cairo. He had been away three weeks.

A fortnight later Nkomo returned to the Middle East, revisiting Cairo, this time for the All African Peoples' Conference. He returned from another trip abroad just before Sandys revisited Salisbury for further constitutional discussions in May 1961. Nkomo and NDP failed to dissuade Sandys from going ahead with the proposals agreed to in February. In June Nkomo had talks with Kaunda in Northern Rhodesia. In July he attended a conference at Winneba, near Accra, organized by the Ghanaian governing party. In August Nkomo returned to London where he met the Duke of Devonshire, junior minister at the Commonwealth Relations Office. Later in the month Nkomo visited Kenyatta in Kenya. Pan-African commitments took Nkomo abroad in September and October, first to Guinea for another meeting of the Steering Committee of the All African Peoples' Organization, and then to Dar-es-Salaam for a PAFMECA summit meeting. In October 1961 Nkomo took a letter from the Secretary of the All African Peoples' Organization, which supported NDP's claims for a constitutional conference, to Macmillan, the British Prime Minister, in London. During this absence from Southern Rhodesia Nkomo paid another visit to Ghana and saw Banda in Nyasaland. Earlier in the year Banda had criticized Nkomo for his part in the constitutional Conference. At this meeting in Nyasaland the two leaders demonstrated their reconciliation. On 10 December 1961 when NDP was banned Nkomo was celebrating Tanganyika's independence in Dar-es-Salaam.

In 1962 Nkomo, now President of the new party, ZAPU, spent little time voluntarily in his homeland. In January, soon after returning from Tanganyika, he embarked on an eleven country tour which kept him away from Southern Rhodesia for three months. In February he went via London to New York to support the proposal that the Committee of Seventeen should consider the Southern Rhodesian question. After returning to London at the beginning of March he flew back to New York when he heard that the Committee of Seventeen was prepared to hear evidence from him. In mid-April he returned to Salisbury.

On 20 May 1962 he addressed a rally in Lusaka and ten days after this arrived in London at the start of another tour which this time lasted two months. Again London was a staging post on the way to New York. Nkomo's activities at the United Nations did not on this occasion include giving evidence to a committee, but consisted only of informal lobbying. During this May-July peregrination he made one of his few journeys into the Communist world when he visited Moscow.

Early in September, just over a month after this second long tour of 1962, Nkomo suddenly went to Dar-es-Salaam. The banning of ZAPU was regarded as imminent and some thought that Nkomo had left Southern Rhodesia to plan a headquarters in exile. A fortnight after leaving for Dar-es-Salaam he moved to Lusaka where he had talks with Kaunda. When the Government did outlaw ZAPU on 20 September Nkomo was still in Lusaka. He delayed his planned return to Salisbury and then secretly disappeared from Northern Rhodesia. He entered Tanganyika by car at Mbeya whence he flew on to Dar-es-Salaam. Although speaking of fresh visits to London and New York, Nkomo stayed in Tanganyika just over a week before finally returning to Salisbury via Nairobi at the beginning of October. On arrival he was immediately restricted for three months to his tribal reserve.

Until January 1963 he therefore had no opportunity for going on foreign excursions. Soon after regaining his freedom he was back in Lusaka for talks with Kaunda and he attended the opening of the Northern Rhodesian Legislative Council. When Butler came to Salisbury late in January as the British Minister responsible for Central Africa Nkomo formed part of a nationalist delegation which spoke to him. In March he again talked to Kaunda in Lusaka and observed Zimbabwe Day (15 March) in Dar-es-Salaam. On 19 March he arrived in London to put his point of view to Butler before the official talks on Federation began, for he was not invited to these. From London he paid a short visit to New

York where he spoke to the Committee of Twenty-four. Returning through London he saw Kaunda who had come for the discussions on Federation. On 28 March 1963 he was in Dar-es-Salaam, nominally the overseas headquarters of the banned ZAPU, where he stayed three days and had talks with Nyerere. Then he returned home in order to appear in court on 1 April, but within less than a fortnight he was leading a flight of the ZAPU executive into exile in Dar-es-Salaam. On 22 April he continued his travels, visiting Cairo, Accra and Liberia before meeting several of his ZAPU colleagues at Addis Ababa for the Pan-African Conference in May 1963 which established the Organization of African Unity. After the Conference Nkomo returned to Dar-es-Salaam where he waited a fortnight in vain for Sithole to join him. Then in mid-June he went home. Later in the month he went to Lusaka to see Kaunda, and to Livingstone to be near the scene of the meeting at Victoria Falls which dismantled the Federation. He was back in Salisbury by 8 July when Sithole and his three supporters in Dar-es-Salaam denounced Nkomo for, *inter alia*, spending too much time out of Southern Rhodesia.

Nkomo at home, 1963 onwards

Nkomo denied that he had wasted time outside the country and many nationalists seemed to agree with him. But it is perhaps significant that Nkomo did not choose to leave Southern Rhodesia after the split. Between July 1963 and April 1964 he voluntarily abstained from foreign intercourse. During this period his obligations to various courts may have helped dissuade him from leaving the country. Four times he had to appear in courts charged with political crimes. On at least one occasion one condition of bail while his appeal against sentence was pending was that he must not leave the country without a magistrate's permission. Since April 1964 Nkomo has been restricted by the Government, and thus unable to go abroad.

9
Evaluation

The overseas activities of the Southern Rhodesian African nationalists have been extensive, but have accomplished little. Just as the nationalists achieved nothing more at home than the support of the African public, so they achieved nothing more abroad than the support of world opinion. Neither their internal nor their external political work shook the European minority's grasp on political power. To what extent was this failure the result of the nationalists' failing to concentrate their hopes and energies on domestic politics?

Background to international activities: domestic frustration

In justification of the Southern Rhodesian Africans' heavy investment of manpower in international relations one must emphasize the basic strategy underlying much of this activity and the formidable difficulties impeding action in Southern Rhodesia. Much, although by no means all, the overseas activity was directed to persuading the British Government to make the Southern Rhodesian Government concede the nationalists' demands. Political work at home was partly an attempt, increasingly vain, to move the territorial Government by immediate pressure, and partly an attempt to create the kind of political atmosphere which would move the British Government to action and which was consequently an aid to the nationalists' endeavours abroad. International political activity beame increasingly attractive as the domestic situation grew worse and showed fewer hopes of success. Few environments can have proved more daunting to political aspirants than Southern Rhodesia to the nationalists. By comparison the international scene offered fairer prospects. If the final frustrations were similar the encouragement the nationalists received abroad was strikingly different from the obstacles they met at home.

Nationalist agitation in Southern Rhodesia made very little impact on the Government. Whitehead made a few reforms, like opening the Civil Service to Africans on equal terms, but only after he had banned one nationalist party, ANC, detained its leaders and introduced repressive legislation. By the time Whitehead instituted these mild reforms the nationalists' mood as a result of their harsh treatment by the Government had hardened and they were demanding far more radical changes. In 1961 the Whitehead Government did agree to modify the Constitution so that some Africans could serve in the legislature, but significantly this agreement did not come without the intervention of the British Government. Once again the changes which a few years before would have seemed revolutionary to the Africans were now regarded by NDP as quite inadequate. The 1961 Constitution was the only major concession made by the Southern Rhodesian Government. Whitehead's party promised to amend the Land Apportionment Act piece by piece until it disappeared, but it was defeated by the blatant white supremacists in the Rhodesian Front, which has ruled since December 1962. This Government, far from compromising with the nationalists (although it did release in January 1963 six ANC leaders who had been held by White-head's regime since February 1959), threatened to modify the Constitution in a way which would have weakened the nationalists' chances of affecting the political system, even if they had chosen to contest elections instead of boycotting them. More important, the Rhodesian Front pressed hard for complete independence from Britain, by negotiations if possible, without if necessary. The Rhodesian Government wished to guarantee its power by obtaining sovereignty. The British Government would grant independence only if it were satisfied that African educational and political progress would be certain and steady. In November 1965 failure of the two Governments to find an agreed basis for independence induced Smith, the Rhodesian Prime Minister, to declare independence unilaterally. This merely confirmed what had long been absolutely clear : the nationalists would receive no concession from a Government which, even more than its more moderate predecessor, believed that the nationalists were irresponsible, neo-Communist agitators who threatened civilized society.

Throughout its history the modern nationalist movement has had a negligible chance of influencing Government policy, especially on fundamental constitutional questions. This has not prevented its attempting to mobilize the masses. Yet here again the Government proved a strong, relentless enemy. The nationalists have found ranged against them the full forces of an efficient modern state. Political life for the nationalists in Southern Rhodesia has usually been diffi-cult and often virtually impossible. The Government has banned nationalist parties because of alleged violence or danger of violence in February 1959 (ANC), December 1961 (NDP), September 1962 (ZAPU) and August 1964 (PCC and ZANU). When the parties were declared illegal they lost their property and usually their leaders. In February 1959 over 300 were arrested and the last six to be released left prison only in 1963. In September 1962 the leaders were restricted for three month periods to their home areas. In August 1964 all the leaders in the country who had not already been immobilized, like Nkomo himself, were restricted and have not been released. For long periods the nationalists, while keeping their faith, had no party. Between February 1959 and January 1960 there was a hiatus, and between September 1962 and July 1963 another gap. Since August 1964 there has been no legal nationalist party in Southern Rhodesia. When ZAPU was banned the nationalists did not form another party because they knew that the Government would sooner or later kill it. ZAPU continued in name and spirit at home and actively only abroad. Only the doubts of some about the wisdom of having no visible party led to the formation of ZANU in August 1963, to which Nkomo replied by forming PCC. Since August 1964 no party has been conceivable because all potential leaders are in the Government's hands or abroad.

Even while the Government allowed the nationalist parties legal existence their lives were precarious. The threat of the Government's paralysing a party by immediate executive action hung over the heads of the nationalists. In addition the Government had and used other weapons against the nationalists which hindered their political advance. NDP, for example, was not permitted to hold meetings in the Reserves, but only in the townships and African Purchase Areas. After the Government referendum in July 1961 to find the opinion of the voters on the proposed constitution the Prime Minister demonstrated the Government's control over political activity by declaring a moratorium on all political meetings in the territory for a week. When ZANU held its first annual Congress in Gwelo in May 1964 the Government supervised the proceedings by instructing the police to attend the meetings of the Congress and by forbidding a mass rally which had been planned. The police regularly listened to the nationalists' speeches and often recorded them in case anything said infringed the numerous laws about political activity. These laws, like the Law and Order (Maintenance) Act, introduced in 1960, and reinforced several times since, made the nationalists very vulnerable to official interference. Several leaders were accused of crimes under these laws. Some avoided punishment after lengthy litigation. Others served sentences, like Enos Nkala, a firebrand member of the NDP executive, who spent two years in prison between 1961 and 1963.

General assessment of international activities

Facing so vigilant, zealous and efficient a government the nationalists naturally sought political channels outside their own country. It was undoubtedly prudent for them to take their fight abroad, but the question remains whether they diverted too many of their resources in men and money into international ventures. This must be answered with the alternative courses of action in mind. Where else could the efforts expended abroad have been profitably employed? The short answer is: nowhere with any guarantee of greater success than was in fact achieved by the actual distribution of energies. More intensive and extensive organization of the masses, greater demonstrations of strength and determination might possibly have budged the Government, but it is unlikely. Widespread sabotage, revolution, or civil war, if any could have been successfully organized, would have offered the best chance of success, either directly by forcing the Government to yield, or indirectly by creating conditions of violence and disturbance which would have brought United Nations or British intervention. However, the nationalist leaders might have doubted, and perhaps rightly, their own ability to organize a large scale, coordinated campaign of violence and the willingness of many Africans in Southern Rhodesia to take the risks necessary for success. In addition some nationalists would have had moral scruples which would have prevented their ready acceptance of a policy of violence. Against an efficient police state like Southern Rhodesia revolutionaries would have had a gigantic task. For these various reasons revolution, or something similar, was not an obviously feasible alternative policy to international activities. In any case, any revolution from within would benefit from that part of the work abroad which aims at providing arms and trained men for guerilla warfare.

The Southern Rhodesian nationalist movement has been inevitably destined to frustration. Every avenue open to them was likely to prove a cul-de-sac. Yet some courses of action were less hopeless than others and some of their international activities, even allowing for the unpromising character of the alternatives, wasted leaders who could have been more usefully employed. Sometimes the Southern Rhodesian Africans showed weak political judgment in their operations abroad. Their ends were only vaguely conceived, or, if precisely conceived, inefficiently pursued. On the other hand, the nationalists sometimes approached their tasks abroad with energy and prudence and the ultimate failure of their international efforts was by no means solely their own fault.

The effects of the leaders' absences abroad

Nkomo's long and frequent absences abroad certainly deprived the nationalist movement in Southern Rhodesia of its acknowledged head and one of its most effective speakers. But at the times when nationalist political activity was legal in Southern Rhodesia many leaders, some rivalling Nkomo in oratory, some his superior in organizational ability, remained in the country to fight the Government while Nkomo and others were doing what they could abroad. On the other hand, the psychological effects on the nationalist rank and file of Nkomo's eagerness to remove the ZAPU executive abroad when the party was banned may have seriously affected the efficiency and enthusiasm of those who were prepared to be persuaded to engage in underground nationalist activities. Nkomo's sudden disappearance just before ZAPU was outlawed in September 1962 and his apparent reluctance to return to face Government action after the ban seem to have shaken the faith of some Southern Rhodesian nationalists. The voluntary exile of nearly the whole executive in April 1963 again undermined the confidence of many Africans, already disappointed by the constant victories of the Government against their movement, and left them leaderless. The reluctance of Nkomo to spend much time in Southern Rhodesia in 1962 and the first part of 1963 contributed to the discontent with his leadership which caused the split in the movement in July 1963. This break, still unrepaired, has undoubtedly lowered the prestige of the Southern Rhodesian nationalist movement in the eyes of foreign observers and weakened it as a fighting force.

The posting of prominent leaders overseas facilitated divisions within the movement. Takawira's absence in London in February 1961 prevented his discussing with Nkomo NDP's agreement to the constitutional proposals which resulted from the Salisbury Conference. As Takawira was isolated from the rest of the executive he expressed his disagreement with Nkomo in violent terms. Furthermore, he gave the text of his hostile telegram to the press. If he had been in Salisbury there would have been no telegram and in any case other members of the executive would have dissuaded Takawira from this action which threatened the unity of the party. The split of July 1963 was far more serious for the nationalist movement than Takawira's indiscretion, which was soon left behind without permanent damage to the cause. The rift between Nkomo and Sithole, like the clash between Nkomo and Takawira, was partly the product of sending part of the executive abroad. Communication between Nkomo and Chikerema in Salisbury and Sithole and his supporters in Dar-es-Salaam was not easy. When the strain between the rival factions became critical they were separated by a thousand miles and mutual denunciation came easier than reconciliation. In Dar-es-Salaam Sithole, Mugabe, Takawira and Malianga unseated Nkomo by a majority decision of the seven executive members present. If the executive had not been dispersed abroad, and if all had met regularly in Southern Rhodesia between April and July 1963, the dissidents might have been contained within ZAPU. At least Nkomo could have met any challenge to his leadership in person and, if there had been a vote of no-confidence, his supporters would have outnumbered the four malcontents on the executive.

To be put in the other side of the balance is the enhanced status which the nationalist leaders gained in the eyes of their supporters from apparently grand deeds in London, New York and other capitals abroad. To Africans who know life only in their local community a political leader who constantly flew from conference to conference seemed to have vast experience. Travel abroad, like higher education, was the privilege of few Africans from Southern Rhodesia and conferred authority on those who had enjoyed it. Even long absences may have contributed to the standing of the

127

leaders. The vast enthusiasm which greeted Nkomo on his return from his longest exiles is comparable to the welcome given Banda when he returned to lead his people after an even longer absence. A kind of mystique attaches to a returning exile. He is less familiar to the masses than the resident leader who is seen and heard every week. By his very strangeness the absentee inspires hope of miraculous solutions. Arrival at an airport is more dramatic than release from prison and may make more of an emotional impact on the waiting crowd. Not many who have faith will ask what the leader has achieved in foreign places.

One might expect that the leaders' experience abroad would have injected new ideas into the theories of the Southern Rhodesian nationalists. Yet before they had travelled extensively overseas, their propaganda contained Western notions of natural rights, quasi-Marxist denunciations of imperialism and Pan-African shibboleths of African brotherhood. It is, of course, difficult to estimate the impact of experience abroad on ideology, but it seems probable that the international relations of the Southern Rhodesian nationalists in the main only strengthened existing convictions.

Relations with the British Government

The most important sphere of overseas activities, because potentially the most rewarding, was Britain. The nationalists' attempts to enlist or compel the support of the British Government were on the whole unsuccessful. They started with the advantage that British Ministers tended to sympathize with Africans' desire for more political power, but with the disadvantage that the British Government was sensitive to the demands of the white Rhodesians with whom a sizeable section of the British political public felt some kinship. Furthermore, the Southern Rhodesian Africans were pitting their inexperience in negotiating against the practised political skills of Ministers like Sandys, Butler and Wilson. The British Government respected the conventions which excluded it from interfering with the Southern Rhodesian Government, which possessed a *de facto* power that the British Government acknowledged. No British Government was prepared to take any risks to help the nationalists against the Southern Rhodesian Government. NDP and its successors fought manfully in the face of these handicaps, but after an encouraging victory the nationalists out-manoeuvred themselves. Having helped to persuade the British Government to call the constitutional Conference at the beginning of 1961, NDP made a disastrous tactical error by accepting the constitutional proposals at the Salisbury Conference, but rejecting them soon after it. If Nkomo and Sithole had refused to accept fifteen seats out of sixty-five at the Conference, they might have forced Sandys to yield them more in order to reach some settlement. Alternatively, if no agreement had emerged from the Conference the nationalists would have earned the reputation of steely determination or extremist stubbornness, either of which might have strengthened their hand in future discussions with the British Government. As it was, the leaders at the Conference agreed to try a constitution which most of the party would not accept. To the British Government the NDP leaders appeared to have no authority over their followers. In any case the psychological moment for influencing the British Government was at the Conference, when Sandys spent a long time discussing the franchise and representation proposals with the nationalists. Once an agreement had been published, the British Government did not feel inclined to give way to further pressure from one of the contending parties. The British Government had already

129

I

gone beyond its usual passive policy to Southern Rhodesia by persuading the Government to come to a conference with the nationalists whom they regarded as mere agitators, and to make constitutional concessions startlingly liberal by traditional European standards in Central Africa. Seemingly through ignorance of what compromise their party would tolerate, Nkomo and the other representatives at the Conference failed to secure the maximum advantage from this unique opportunity. Afterwards the nationalists naturally kept demanding a fresh constitutional conference, although the British Government never looked like granting the request. After the success of the Rhodesian Front at the first election under the new Constitution the likelihood of a constitutional conference under British chairmanship became more remote, for it was inconceivable that the new, more right wing Government would agree to come to any constitutional conference which might modify the political system to the advantage of the Africans. The British Government believed that they must act realistically and consult the Southern Rhodesian Government about any proposed political changes for the territory, so no British Prime Minister was likely to call a constitutional conference which only those outside the Southern Rhodesian Government would attend. The situation was desperate for the nationalists. They could scarcely be blamed, however, for clinging to the hope that they might shift the British Government. It was a minute chance, but if the gamble came off the dividends might be large. In this case a policy at odds with realism was justified. If, however, as seems the case on the surface, the Southern Rhodesian nationalists believed their relation to the British Government was closely analogous to that of nationalists in ordinary colonies, they were deceiving themselves. The British Government did not regard itself as having the same rights and powers to promote political change in Southern Rhodesia as it had in Northern Rhodesia. It is doubtful if the Southern Rhodesian nationalists always realized the weakness of their position in arguing with the British Government. In the role of petitioners they were perhaps ill-advised to rail at the British Government. General threats of imminent widespread violence which never fully materialized and fierce invective against those from whom concessions were sought were not the tactics calculated to win ground from British Ministers who had nothing to fear from resisting the Africans but the ineffective obloquy of their sympathizers.

Winning support abroad

Much of the nationalists' work abroad consisted in convincing others of the justice of their case. This work was most justified at the beginning of each propaganda campaign, when the Africans from Southern Rhodesia were trying to create or activate the interest of a state or organization in their predicament. To continue the efforts of persuasion when the ally was won or when his support had proved itself impotent was ill-judged. Nkomo's early tours of potentially sympathetic countries in 1959 and 1960 contributed to a world-wide consciousness of the Southern Rhodesian situation. Similarly, the first few visits to the United Nations probably won new friends. But so much of the Southern Rhodesian Africans' missionary work was preaching to the converted. It took little to convince states which had been colonies or were Communists dedicated to fight imperialism that the Southern Rhodesian nationalists' cause was just. The United Nations Organization and the Pan-African organizations did not need constant reminding by Nkomo and his colleagues to pass appropriate resolutions condemning Britain and Southern

Rhodesia. There probably came a point where the Southern
Rhodesian Africans' troubles became more valuable to Pan-
Africanism as a rallying cry than Pan-Africanism was to
the Southern Rhodesian nationalists as an ally. The nationalists congratulated Nkomo and the others on 'victories' at
the United Nations and at Pan-African conferences, and
did not seem to recognize the emptiness of these victories.
The imperviousness of Britain to international criticism
should have become clear to the Southern Rhodesian nationalists through experience. They could have economized
drastically in their export of men.

It is doubtful whether the offices in various capitals always justified their existence. Was there sufficient work in
London or Lusaka, let alone Cairo and Accra, to provide a
representative with constant employment useful to the
nationalist movement? The representatives often moved
on the periphery of power politics. The apparent futility
of such politics in exile may even have created in the minds
of hosts and observers an impression that the Southern
Rhodesian nationalist movement as a whole was impotent.
Governments with similar ideologies would support the
nationalists in public, but privately they might think
them a poor investment politically or financially.

In England and Northern Rhodesia (and elsewhere) many
of the Southern Rhodesian nationalist leaders have not im-
pressed those whom they met as shrewd, dynamic or self-
less leaders. Some of their critics may not always have
made allowances, when judging the Southern Rhodesian
nationalists, for their unique difficulties. That they were
ineffective compared with most other African nationalists
and often begging for help abroad was liable to be attributed
to their characters as much as to their conditions. Nkomo
himself aroused audiences by his speeches (even the Conservative Parliamentary Commonwealth Committee), but

he seemed to lack other important political qualities. Retrospectively, he appears often not to have known what he wanted, why he was doing things or what he would do next. It looks as if he responded pragmatically to each event and audience without concern for consistency and without reference to a general plan of action. This indecisiveness may have communicated itself to nationalist leaders in other countries who met him from time to time on his travels.

Friends made abroad did not enable the Southern Rhodesian nationalists to gain power at home, but they helped sustain the nationalists' propaganda and protest. PAFMECSA might have devoted its resources, admittedly slight, to helping the Southern Rhodesian Africans for a year as it did for Kaunda's UNIP in Northern Rhodesia in 1962. The OAU Liberation Committee has contributed money and arms, although Pan-African organizations tend to be handicapped in the practical aid they can give to still struggling nationalists by the poverty of the member states. Militarily the independent African states are too weak to risk war on behalf of parties like ZAPU against such relatively powerful states as Southern Rhodesia. The money that the Southern Rhodesian nationalists obtained from sympathizers was particularly useful to the movement when the parties were banned at home and no dues were coming in from rank and file members. Yet the income from foreign sources must be offset against the expenditure on foreign travel and organization abroad.

The military training for guerillas and the supply of offensive materials might prove to be the most important gains from international activity. So far the nationalists' guerilla strength has been mainly latent, possibly dormant. The task of making it effective is immense. The nationalist leaders still at liberty abroad are politicians, not generals, yet revolution needs leaders with military skills and experience. The Rhodesian nationalist leaders in Lusaka have tried to plan a few guerilla expeditions into Rhodesia, but they are too remote from the scene of hostilities to exercise control once the men have left Lusaka. Yet if the leaders themselves were to move the headquarters of the para-military expeditions to Rhodesia itself, they would run a serious risk of capture and this would deprive the nationalist movement of the few leaders still left to conduct the fight against the Government. If those Africans trained abroad are to be successful, they need active cooperation from Africans who are sympathetic but who have stayed in Rhodesia. But most of these have not reacted strongly to the challenge of UDI or to the calls from the exiled nationalists. With a shortage of jobs those in employment will tend to avoid radical commitment to a political cause with an uncertain future. The Government has deliberately let the Africans know how strong it is. Many Africans seem cowed by long experience of being treated as inferiors by Europeans. As in South Africa the Africans, although sympathetic to nationalism, do not look to be in a revolutionary mood.

The nationalists' motives in overseas work

Finally, what motives, other than their ostensible and declared ones, had the nationalists in looking abroad, in going abroad and in staying abroad? Crippled at home by the Government, the leaders felt the need to do something positive somewhere. The Government could not easily prevent the nationalists from meeting foreign politicians in other countries, although they could try to stop the nationalists from leaving Southern Rhodesia. To keep up the enthusiasm of their frustrated supporters the nationalist leaders needed to give the appearance of taking decisive action. Their more spectacular exploits abroad satisfied this need.

Nkomo himself spent so much time abroad until mid-1963 that it is difficult not to infer that he enjoyed political missions abroad. He may have felt a sense of power from moving among those who actually had the sort of power he wanted. While he was out of Southern Rhodesia he was treated with courtesy. In his own country, although worshipped by his supporters, he was followed by the police and, like all Africans in the territory, constantly humiliated by ubiquitous discrimination.

Nkomo seems to have been reluctant, too, to return to Southern Rhodesia if the Government was likely to restrict or detain him. He went back in 1960 only after Whitehead had publicly announced that he would not arrest and imprison him. When ZAPU was banned in 1962 Nkomo delayed his intended return to Southern Rhodesia. The Government was restricting the ZAPU leaders to their home districts and Nkomo may have thought that he could be more use to the movement in freedom abroad. Also Nkomo seems to have believed for part of the time he spent abroad after ZAPU was banned that the Government might ill-treat him if he returned. His slowness to return home on these two occasions may be attributed to fear or prudence or a mixture of both.

Other Southern Rhodesian nationalists have left the territory or stayed out of it because they know that the Government would in some way restrict their movements if they returned. Since August 1964 this has been true of all the nationalist leaders. Incarceration has commonly formed an essential part of African nationalists' apprenticeship as national leaders and this has been true in Southern Rhodesia. But there the danger has existed several times that the nationalist movements might suffer paralysis because its leaders were locked up. Silundika has argued that free men are more useful to the movement than martyrs. Now exile is the only escape from martyrdom.

Suggestions for further reading

Source books and books referred to in the text are included in this list of further reading on Southern Rhodesian African nationalism and its political contexts.

Books

The book by Nathan Shamuyarira is the only one primarily about Southern Rhodesian African nationalism.

CLEGG, E., *Race and Politics: Partnership in the Federation of Rhodesia and Nyasaland*, Oxford University Press, 1960.

A study of race relations in the Federation, with particular emphasis on Northern Rhodesia.

COX, R., *Pan-Africanism in Practice: PAFMECSA 1958–1964*, Oxford University Press, 1964.

A useful brief history of PAFMECSA.

CREIGHTON, T. R. M., *The Anatomy of Partnership: Southern Rhodesia and the Central African Federation*, Faber and Faber, 1960.

A study of the Federation, Southern Rhodesia and the place of Southern Rhodesia in the Federation. Mr Creighton includes a very short section on the Southern Rhodesian ANC and reprints the ANC statement of principles, policy and programme.

DUNN, C., *Central African Witness*, Gollancz, 1959.

Mr Dunn, an *Observer* correspondent, drawing readily on his own experience, argues that the leaders of the Federation tried to preserve European domination.

FRANCK, T. M., *Race and Nationalism: the Struggle for Power in Rhodesia-Nyasaland*, Allen and Unwin, 1960.

Professor Franck discusses the achievements, problems and future of the Federation. He has a short section on the influences on the Southern Rhodesian ANC.

GRAY, R., *The Two Nations: Aspects of the Development of Race Relations in the Rhodesias and Nyasaland*, Oxford University Press, 1960.

Mr Gray deals with his subject up to 1953 and includes a most valuable history of the origins of African political awareness in Southern Rhodesia.

HANNA, A. J., *The Story of the Rhodesias and Nyasaland*, Faber and Faber, 1960.

A helpful introduction to the history of British Central Africa.

LEGUM, C. (ed.), *Africa: a Handbook to the Continent*, Anthony Blond, 1961.

Contains a short section on Southern Rhodesian politics and some biographical notes on some of the nationalists.

LEYS, C., *European Politics in Southern Rhodesia*, Oxford University Press, 1959.

The standard authority on its subect. Events since it was written have not invalidated most of its conclusions.

LEYS, C. and PRATT, R. C. (ed.), *A New Deal in Central Africa*, Heinemann, 1960.

A stimulating series of articles by several writers hostile to the Federation as it worked out. They explain the history of the Federation, discuss arguments about it, and make recommendations for its reform.

PALLEY, C., *The Constitutional History and Law of Southern Rhodesia 1888–1965*, Oxford University Press, 1966.

This most scholarly book is the definitive work on its subject.

RANGER, T. O., *Crisis in Southern Rhodesia*, Fabian Commonwealth Bureau, 1960.

A Fabian pamphlet analysing the political situation in Southern Rhodesia in 1960 and arguing that the British Government should actively help the nationalists. It contains some useful material on the nationalists.

SANGER, C., *Central African Emergency*, Heinemann, 1960.

Mr Sanger, a *Guardian* correspondent, argues the case of Africans in Central Africa against the white governments, and considers the future of the Federation. There are a few pages on Southern Rhodesian African nationalism.

SEGAL, R. M., *Political Africa: a Who's Who of Personalities and Parties*, Stevens, 1961.

Contains information on Southern Rhodesian African nationalism and short biographies of some of its leaders.

SHAMUYARIRA, N. M., *Crisis in Rhodesia*, Andre Deutsch, 1965.

Mr Shamuyarira, a ZANU leader, has been a newspaper editor and a university lecturer during the rise and decline of African nationalism in Southern Rhodesia. His book, partly based on personal experience, is primarily a description of African nationalism in his country. It is not strictly an academic study, but it is an intelligent and informed account by one passionately committed to the nationalist cause.

SITHOLE, N., *African Nationalism*, Oxford University Press, 1959.

Rev. Sithole, the ZANU President, completed this book by the end of 1957, before he became an active nationalist leader. He sympathetically explains African nationalism in general (not the Southern Rhodesian movement in particular).

SYMONDS, J., *Southern Rhodesia: Background to Crisis*, Oxford University Press, 1965.

In this booklet the Secretary of the Africa Bureau provides the information necessary for understanding the then threatened UDI.

TODD, J., *Rhodesia*, Macgibbon and Kee, 1966.

A vivid and emotional condemnation of Southern Rhodesian white society by Garfield Todd's daughter. She writes a little on the African nationalists, partly from personal experience.

WISEMAN, H. V., *Britain and the Commonwealth*, Allen and Unwin, 1965.
A useful introduction to its subject.

Articles

RANGER, T. O., 'Prospects for Race Relations in Southern Rhodesia', *Race Relations Journal*, xxvii, no. 2, April-June 1960, 69-81.
Contains valuable argument and information on African nationalism in Southern Rhodesia.

RANGER, T. O., 'Some Attitudes to African Nationalism : a Study of Writing in English about African Nationalism with Special Reference to Central Africa' (paper presented to the Leverhulme History Conference, Salisbury, Southern Rhodesia, September 1960).
In arguing that many white academics interpret African nationalism with an imperialist bias, Prof Ranger criticizes Prof Franck's views in *Race and Nationalism* on Southern Rhodesian African nationalism, and provides useful information on the movement.

ROTBERG, R., 'From Moderate to Militant', *Africa Report*, vii, no. 3, March 1962, 3-4, 8, 22.
A short biography of Nkomo.

VAN VELSEN, J., 'Trends in African Nationalism in Southern Rhodesia', *Kroniek van Afrika*, ii, June 1964, 139-157.
A good survey of the development of African nationalism in Southern Rhodesia.

Official Government Publications

(i) Southern Rhodesia

Review Tribunal [Preventive Detention (Temporary Provisions) Act 1959] General Report, C.S.R. 27—1959 [Beadle Report].
The Southern Rhodesian Government published this Report of the Tribunal set up to consider the activities of ANC. In arguing that ANC was a subversive and dangerous organization, the Report provides some information on the party.

(ii) United Kingdom

Report of the Nyasaland Commission of Inquiry, Cmnd. 814, 1959 [Devlin Report].

The British Government published this Report of the Commission set up to report on the disturbances in Nyasaland, 1958–1959. It contains an authoritative history of nationalism in Nyasaland.

Report of the Southern Rhodesia Constitutional Conference, Salisbury, Southern Rhodesia, February 1961, Cmnd. 1291, 1961.

This Report contains the proposals for a new constitution agreed to by various parties at the Conference, including NDP.

Appendix:

Periods of legal existence

September 1957–February 1959	African National Congress	– ANC
January 1960–December 1961	National Democratic Party	– NDP
December 1961–September 1962	Zimbabwe African People's Union	– ZAPU
August 1963–August 1964	People's Caretaker Council	– PCC
	Zimbabwe African National Union	– ZANU

PCC called itself ZAPU overseas

143

For Product Safety Concerns and Information please contact our EU
representative GPSR@taylorandfrancis.com
Taylor & Francis Verlag GmbH, Kaufingerstraße 24, 80331 München, Germany